KNOCK IT DOWN OR DO IT UP?

Sustainable house building: New build and refurbishment in the Sustainable Communities Plan

The College of Estate Management research team:
> Frances Plimmer
> Gaye Pottinger
> Sarah Harris
> Michael Waters
> Yasmin Pocock

With additional input from:
> Philip Leverton
> Henry Russell
> Adrian Smith

  The College of Estate Management

This work has been partly funded by BRE Trust. Any views expressed are not necessarily those of BRE Trust. While every effort is made to ensure the accuracy and quality of information and guidance when it is first published, BRE Trust can take no responsibility for the subsequent use of this information, nor for any errors or omissions it may contain.

The mission of BRE Trust is 'Through education and research to promote and support excellence and innovation in the built environment for the benefit of all'. Through its research programmes the Trust aims to achieve:
- a higher quality built environment
- built facilities that offer improved functionality and value for money
- a more efficient and sustainable construction sector, with
- a higher level of innovative practice.

A further aim of the Trust is to stimulate debate on challenges and opportunities in the built environment.

BRE Trust
Garston, Watford, Herts WD25 9XX
Tel: 01923 664598
Email: secretary@bretrust.co.uk
www.bretrust.org.uk

BRE Trust, a company limited by guarantee, registered in England and Wales (no. 3282856) and registered as a charity in England (no. 1092193) and in Scotland (no. SC039320).
Registered Office: Bucknalls Lane, Garston, Watford, Herts WD25 9XX

BRE Trust and BRE publications are available from
www.ihsbrepress.com
or
IHS BRE Press
Willoughby Road, Bracknell RG12 8FB
Tel: 01344 328038
Fax: 01344 328005
Email: brepress@ihs.com

Published by IHS BRE Press for BRE Trust

Requests to copy any part of this publication should be made to the publisher:
IHS BRE Press, Garston, Watford WD25 9XX
Tel: 01923 664761
Email: brepress@ihs.com

Printed on paper sourced from responsibly managed forests

FB 16
© **The College of Estate Management, Reading**
First published 2008
ISBN 978-1-84806-020-3

CONTENTS

FIGURES

TABLES AND CASE STUDIES

ACRONYMS

AAP	Area action plan
BCIS	Building Cost Information Service
BSI	British Standards Institution
C&D	Construction and demolition
CABE	Commission for Architecture and the Built Environment
CAR	Cambridge Architectural Research
CHP	Combined heat and power
CIOB	Chartered Institute of Building
CPO	Compulsory purchase order
CPRE	Campaign to Protect Rural England (formerly Council for the Preservation of Rural England)
DCLG	Department of Communities and Local Government
DCMS	Department for Culture, Media and Sport
DEFRA	Department of the Environment, Food and Rural Affairs
DETR	Department for the Environment, Transport and the Regions (no longer in existence, with many of the department's responsibilities now covered by the DCLG and the Department for Transport)
DoE	Department of the Environment (no longer in existence, with responsibilities now largely covered by DEFRA)
DTI	Department of Trade and Industry (now Department for Business, Enterprise and Regulatory Reform)
DTLR	Department for Transport, Local Government and the Regions (no longer in existence, with responsibilities now covered by the DCLG)
EST	Energy Saving Trust
EU	European Union
HBF	Home Builders Federation
HLF	Heritage Lottery Fund
HMR	Housing market renewal
KPI	Key performance indicator

LCC	Life cycle costs
LCCA	Life cycle cost analysis
MMC	Modern methods of construction
MtC	Million tonnes of carbon
NRA	Neighbourhood renewal assessment
ODPM	Office of the Deputy Prime Minister (no longer in existence, with responsibilities now covered by the DCLG)
PFI	Private finance initiative
PPG15	Planning Policy Guidance 15: Planning and the Historic Environment, published September 1994
PPG16	Planning Policy Guidance 16: Archaeology and Planning, published November 1990
PPS1	Planning Policy Statement 1: Delivering Sustainable Development, published February 2005 (this replaced Planning Policy Guidance Note 1: General Policies and Principles [PPG1], published in February 1997)
PPS22	Planning Policy Statement 22: Renewable Energy, published August 2004
PPS3	Planning Policy Statement 3: Housing, published November 2006 (this replaced Planning Policy Guidance Note 3: Housing [PPG3], published in March 2000)
PRT	Prince's Regeneration Trust
RICS	Royal Institution of Chartered Surveyors
RTH	Regeneration Through Heritage
SAP	Standard Assessment Procedure (for energy rating of dwellings)
SAVE	Save Britain's Heritage
SCP	Sustainable Communities Plan
SDC	Sustainable Development Commission
SPAB	Society for the Protection of Ancient Buildings
SRI	Socially responsible investment
SUR	Sustainable urban regeneration
WLCA	Whole life costing analysis

ACKNOWLEDGEMENTS

The authors have produced this research report independently, and the views expressed are our own.

The research team would like to thank the following for their help and support:

* the BRE Trust, for sponsoring this research and assisting in some aspects of the data collection and sourcing of commercially sensitive data;
* members of the steering group for this project, which included:
    – John Burdett, Secretary and Research Manager to the BRE Trust
    – Tim Yates, Technical Director, BRE
    – Ashley Dabson, acting Director of Research, The College of Estate Management
* those who contributed information and material to the research; and, finally,
* the survey respondents, who, for reasons of confidentiality, must remain anonymous.

Research Department
The College of Estate Management
Whiteknights
Reading RG6 6AW
Tel: +44 (0) 118 921 4696
Fax: +44 (0) 118 921 4620

FOREWORD

Over the last 60 years, the UK has seen an almost total decline in manufacturing and heavy industry, with concomitant and radical changes in community health, structure and supporting infrastructure. The perception of the UK today is of a post-industrial society, and such societies demand different functions of their urban centres.

Some see ways of achieving physical regeneration through clearance and rebuilding, others look to refurbish existing buildings. Both methods have implications for the communities within and around the areas proposed for regeneration, as well as for the overall sustainability of the schemes in financial, environmental and social terms.

This BRE Trust Report focuses on government policy as expressed in the Sustainable Communities Plan. This Plan was developed to provide a long-term strategy for delivering sustainable communities while tackling housing supply issues in both areas of high demand (predominantly in the South East) and low demand (in areas such as the North West). The dilemma of whether it is better to 'knock it down' or 'do it up' has re-emerged in the housing market renewal or 'pathfinder' areas that were established as part of the Sustainable Communities Plan. Stakeholders in these localities are therefore trying to decide how best to both regenerate the housing stock and create sustainable communities.

This report describes the long-standing debate between those who believe that the demolition of a high proportion of the existing housing stock is an essential part of urban regeneration, and those who believe that retention is the key part of any sustainable regeneration programme.

Whichever approach proves most beneficial for a particular area, the overriding objective, for both public and private sectors, must be to achieve healthy, active and thriving communities which are sustainable in the long term.

Ann Heywood PhD BSc FRICS FRGS MCMI
Principal
The College of Estate Management
Whiteknights
Reading
Berkshire RG6 6AW

Tel: 0118 921 4643
Fax: 0118 986 9878
Email: a.heywood@cem.ac.uk

ABOUT THE COLLEGE OF ESTATE MANAGEMENT

Founded in 1919, The College of Estate Management is the leading international body providing distance learning education, training and research to the property professions and construction industry. Its courses are designed to help students obtain professional qualifications, develop a specialisation, work more effectively and develop lifelong learning skills. Students from over 80 countries are currently registered on College courses.

Research at the College continues to be relevant, well focused on the needs of potential users, responsive to market developments and changing government policy. Important research themes in recent years have therefore included environmental issues, IT and property, sustainability and residential property.

College reports have been influential in guiding government policies in relevant specified areas, such as the Commonhold and Leasehold Reform Act 2002. One report led directly to the development of a new code of practice on valuing for the 2004 Right to Buy housing legislation.

1 INTRODUCTION

1.1 THE RESEARCH COMMISSION

The College of Estate Management carried out this independent research during 2006 and 2007. The project was designed to examine the issues surrounding the sustainability of newly constructed housing, in comparison with the refurbishment of existing housing, in the context of the government's Sustainable Communities Plan. The research was sponsored by the BRE Trust. This section of the report outlines the background to the research and explains the scope of the study in more detail.

1.2 BACKGROUND

The Sustainable Communities Plan (SCP) (ODPM, 2003a) sets out a long-term strategy for delivering sustainable communities while tackling housing supply issues that include areas of high demand in the South East and low demand in areas such as the North West. The plan identifies around 1 million homes affected by low demand and abandonment, spread across over 120 local authorities in the North and Midlands. It establishes nine market renewal pathfinder (housing market renewal) areas to tackle problems in the most deprived areas of the country and incorporating about half of the homes affected by low demand, with the intention of replacing obsolete housing with modern sustainable accommodation, through demolition, new building or refurbishment.

However, there has been criticism of the plans to demolish existing stock and replace it with new-build housing. Some of this has focused on the carbon emissions generated when building new homes, which can be in the region of 9.54 tonnes (tC) per home. With a current build rate of around 140,000 new homes in England per year this could lead to 1.41 MtC being emitted into the atmosphere (Environmental Audit Committee, 2007). Other potential concerns are the sustainability of materials used, such as aggregates and timber, and the amount of waste generated, including contaminated soil and its disposal. For example, the construction industry produces some 70 million tonnes of waste each year in the UK, and new build contributes significantly to carbon dioxide emissions. New house building therefore can create tensions within the sustainable development framework at the heart of the SCP.

Yet around 3.4% of total housing stock lies vacant, including some 200,000 pre-1919 homes. English Heritage (2003) has emphasised that the historic environment has an important role to play in realising the ambitions of reuse and renewal of areas of abandonment and decline in these localities. It is argued that this is especially true of housing in the pathfinder areas – for example, Victorian or Edwardian terraced housing, some of which may be back to back.

Evidence is accumulating to suggest that there is a danger that properties in some areas may be demolished and replaced unnecessarily, with historic heritage being lost (CPRE, 2004; English Heritage, 2005).

However, demolition may be appropriate to remove inadequate housing stock. In the North West, for example, it is likely that large-scale demolition of high-density terraced housing will be required (Girling, 2004); whilst the emphasis on new build has important ramifications for energy consumption and waste generation within the sustainable development agenda.

It is therefore necessary to compare the two approaches to housing renewal:
* refurbishment of the existing housing stock; and
* demolition of current properties to be replaced by new buildings.

Various indicators or metrics exist to monitor the sustainability of house building construction standards. For example, BRE's EcoHomes standard (Wain, 2005:11) assesses issues grouped into seven categories: energy; water; pollution; materials; transport; ecology and land use; health and well-being. However, currently, many of the categories are optional.

There is evidence (discussed elsewhere in this report) that, despite the pressure to ensure sustainability in construction (amongst other industries), practices are changing very little, and largely only as a result of legislation rather than industry-led initiatives. Traditional methodologies and traditional products dominate in the market. There are obviously barriers to achieving greater levels of sustainability in construction, which are relevant to the focus of this research.

It is clear that there are arguments for and against refurbishment and new build based on economic, environmental and social grounds. More detailed research is now needed, to critically examine the methodologies for assessing the sustainability of new build and refurbishment schemes in relation to housing, and to understand how they are being applied by the house building industry.

1.3   AIMS/OBJECTIVES

The overall aim of this new research is to assess the sustainability of refurbishing existing housing in comparison with demolishing it and building new housing, jn the context of the government's SCP.

The objectives of the research are as follows:

* to assess the construction sector's attitudes to the sustainability of refurbishing older housing versus demolition and new build;
* to examine the range of methodologies (including whole life cycle costing) available to the house builder to assess the relative sustainability of housing construction and refurbishment;
* to examine the methods actually used by house builders to evaluate the relative sustainability of new-build housing versus refurbishment;
* to investigate the main drivers towards and barriers against housing construction and refurbishment;
* to review the sustainable construction techniques being employed by house builders.

1.4   METHODOLOGY

The research aim and objectives were achieved through a literature review and questionnaire survey.

Literature and policy review

A desktop review was undertaken of the literature/policy guidance and previous research relating to construction and refurbishment of housing, with a particular emphasis on economic/whole life cycle analysis.

National survey

A national survey of house builders, quantity surveyors, development surveyors and architects was conducted to assess attitudes towards and perceptions of sustainable construction, MMC, existing standards of sustainability, and the use of sustainability assessment tool kits.

2 URBAN RENEWAL AND REGENERATION POLICY FRAMEWORK

2.1 INTRODUCTION

The context in which this research is undertaken reflects the UK government's policies of sustainability, specifically its Sustainable Communities Plan and policies to encourage sustainable construction, and also the very urgent problem of dealing with areas of low demand and even abandonment of housing, largely in the Midlands and North of England.

There is therefore a clear mismatch in England between demand for housing in the South East and an overprovision in the Midlands and the North. It is also important to note that, in general, it is older and unmodernised dwellings that are being rejected by the market (although not exclusively so).

Government policy has been to focus on areas of low demand by providing specific funding and focus for achieving a housing-led regeneration initiative. However, the choices facing those responsible for local housing provision in such locations are either to demolish and rebuild, or to refurbish the existing stock. Issues of sustainability underpin this choice. There are also pressures from the construction industry, as well as issues of social acceptability, and the reality of whether such new or refurbished accommodation will be sustainable over its future useful life, which must all be factored in.

This section outlines relevant government policy, as well as providing details of the government's policy for areas of low demand. It therefore provides a context within which the relative advantages and disadvantages of demolish and rebuild, and refurbishment can be discussed.

2.2 SUSTAINABLE COMMUNITIES PLAN

To meet future growth, and achieve sustainable communities, the UK government launched the Sustainable Communities Plan (SCP) in February 2003 (ODPM, 2003b). This is a long-term strategy for delivering sustainable communities in both urban and rural areas. It combines new build within identified growth areas and refurbishment in areas of low demand.

In addition to encouraging growth areas in the South East of England, and also the provision of quality public open space, a particular focus of the SCP is to tackle issues of low demand, specifically in the Midlands and

the North. The areas of low demand were grouped into nine housing market renewal (HMR) pathfinder areas (see Section 2.4):

- Newcastle and Gateshead;
- Hull and the East Riding of Yorkshire;
- South Yorkshire (Sheffield, Doncaster, Barnsley, Rotherham);
- Birmingham and Sandwell;
- North Staffordshire (Stoke, East Newcastle-under-Lyme and East Biddulph);
- Manchester and Salford;
- Merseyside (Liverpool, Sefton and Wirral);
- Oldham and Rochdale; and
- East Lancashire (Burnley, Blackburn, Hyndburn, Pendle and Rossendale).

The drivers behind the SCP in relation to housing are:

1. the perception that there is insufficient accommodation to meet the needs of the projected future population in the regions of England where demand is anticipated, following on from the Barker reviews (Barker, 2003, 2004);
2. the need to ensure sustainable housing (particularly in relation to the existing stock);
3. the opportunities to reduce the large amounts of waste and carbon emissions by reforming the practices of the construction industry, and to regenerate/revitalise areas of low housing demand; and
4. the need to provide renewal of areas of low demand.

Sustainability (Edwards and Turrent, 2000: 20) in terms of housing needs to address five key areas:

- conservation of natural resources (land, energy, water);
- sensible reuse of man-made materials;
- maintenance of ecosystems and their regenerative potential;
- equity between generations, people and classes; and
- provision of health, safety and security.

It is, in particular, in relation to the first two items above that the choice falls between demolish and rebuild or refurbish. The use of resources, both natural and man-made, is important in the context of housing because of the very high energy costs involved in both demolition and construction processes, and also in the loss of 'embodied energy'[1] when existing buildings are destroyed. Although refurbishment may limit the opportunities for redesign, relocating, and responding to the (apparent) needs of the market, this report investigates claims that it does have major advantages in conserving both natural and man-made resources.

Edwards and Turrent (2000: 20) define sustainable housing as:

"… housing that meets the perceived and real needs of the present in a resource efficient fashion, whilst providing attractive, safe and ecologically rich neighbourhoods"

(ODPM, 2003b: 12)

However, various concerns about the SCP have emerged in relation to new build. These views were encapsulated in the 2005 Environmental Audit Committee report (2005), which stated that:

"The urgent need for new housing, if met with undue haste and an absence of thorough environmental appraisals, will lead to significant and effectively irreversible environmental damage."

(Environmental Audit Committee, 2005: 3)

A review by the Sustainability Development Commission (Power, 2004: 2-3) of the SCP, and its connection with sustainable development and communities, raised some critical issues about the fundamental sustainability of the SCP. The most relevant for this study are as follows:

- There is a crucial need to raise energy efficiency to 'excellent' eco-standards in both existing and new homes.
- New uses need to be found for the obsolete urban infrastructure of the older industrial heartlands.
- The SCP does not link the impact of additional supply on demand.
- The SCP does not deal with the power to conserve local affordable stock for local residents and workers.
- The assumption that massive job expansion will fuel demand for housing cannot be taken for granted.
- The SCP does not encourage community involvement or ownership of the proposals.
- It is recognised in the review that large-scale demolition and ambitious building plans are not popular.
- The SCP does not propose tools for delivery.

Despite the apparent gaps in government policy noted by the review, and the emphasis that government and the media have placed on the need to provide large amounts of suitable accommodation to meet the anticipated growth in demand for housing in the South East of England, there remains a need to respond to the social and environmental problems caused by the abandonment of housing in the Midlands and the North of England.

2.3 LOW DEMAND AND ABANDONMENT OF HOUSING

Low-demand localities can be divided into three broad groups (Bramley and Pawson, 2002: 403):

- generic low demand across all tenures, generally of serious magnitude and impact;
- low demand/oversupply of social sector housing accompanied by adequate or buoyant private market conditions; and
- isolated patches of unpopular social housing in generally high-demand areas.

These groups can be defined largely by factual data, but the causes of such a situation are harder to determine and therefore to deal with. (See Section 2.4.3.)

A characteristic of low-demand areas is the abandonment of dwellings and often neighbourhoods:

"Abandonment of property is the process by which residential units … become detached from the housing market in a number of ways and eventually fall into disuse, in effect abandoned by their owners." (Keenan et al., 1999: 705)

It is also clear that the properties affected are in both the public and private sectors (including housing association dwellings); that they range across all tenures; and that some of the properties are in good condition – some even newly constructed – but have never been occupied (Keenan *et al.*, 1999; Bramley and Pawson, 2002: 394–395).

Keenan *et al.* (1999: 705) consider that abandoned properties are a waste of resources, and a major factor contributing to the downward spiral of some inner cities, with a contagion effect, like a 'virus', which can lead to whole neighbourhoods becoming devoid of social and economic activity.

"The appearance of one or two abandoned properties appears to be sufficient to trigger what seemed like a virus, attaching randomly in clearly defined and weakened neighbourhoods." (Keenan et al., 1999: 710)

Their paper discusses literature from the USA, from which it is clear that the root of the problem is the decline and collapse of major industrial sectors. Literature from the UK is virtually non-existent, focusing instead on 'voids' and 'vacants', with abandonment implicit in both situations. Indeed, the authors acknowledge that, only recently (the paper cites *"in the last 18 months or so"*) has the issue become more recognised. Citing more recent research, the paper states (Keenan *et al.*, 1999: 708) that the main causes of abandonment are:

- the depopulation of large cities and the loss of manufacturing jobs;

---

1 'Embodied energy' is a term used to describe the total quantity of energy required to create an item. This includes energy used in mining, processing and refining the item as well as any transport used between each of these stages and the item's final destination (see Section 4.6)

- a chronic mismatch of supply and demand at the local level;
- the unpopularity of neighbourhoods with poor housing or high crime; and
- a rapid increase in the number of people moving in and out of different households.

Thus the symptoms may present the situation as low demand or abandoned dwellings, but the causes are social in origin. The extent to which dealing with the symptoms (eg by refurbishing or replacing the existing housing stock) will solve the problem is a major issue for the success of government policy.

However, the Empty Homes Agency (undated) consider that, in contrast to new house building, where there is no VAT, the VAT applied to repair, maintenance and refurbishment represents a financial disincentive to maintain dwellings and *"is often the root cause that allows homes to fall into disrepair in the first place"*. (For a more detailed discussion of VAT see Section 5.4.)

In discussing the issue of policy, Keenan *et al.* (1999: 710) state that: *"The low demand issue is a graphic illustration of policy failure ... "* with the funding system largely to blame, as local/regional housing authorities and housing associations are reluctant to admit an oversupply in case housing subsidies are redirected to other locations. Another problem identified was that the monitoring systems failed to demonstrate the highly localised problems.

"None of the main housing needs models were disaggregated in a way that could have shown the nascent problem of oversupply of housing in some areas of the country." (ibid: 712)

The impact on communities of low demand for housing has created important sociological problems, including high mobility within local areas (with motives including crime and vandalism, threat of burglary, mounting personal debt, disputes with neighbours, perceptions of nuisance, abusive relationships, overbearing landlords), and the organisation of housing benefit frauds (Keenan *et al.*, 1999).

"... one of the more alarming aspects of low demand for housing is the way in which behaviour may be influenced as the stability of decades of shared life turns to insecurity." (Keenan et al., 1999: 714).

Thus Keenan *et al.* (1999: 714) conclude that:

"The most serious consequence of low demand in the many places affected by it is social turmoil ... a variety of local factors are at work in the creation or otherwise of abandoned housing ... [and, as a result,] more thought needs to be given to the kind of building programme necessary to meet the needs of the projected 4.4 million new households over 25 years to the year 2016."

There is a very clear regional imbalance in the distribution of low-demand areas, with the literature citing such damaged locations as Birmingham, Bradford, Coventry, Leeds, Liverpool, Manchester, Newcastle and Sheffield. While a regional imbalance between the North and the South of England is not new, there is evidence that low demand has occurred in the capital, but that the effects in London have been mitigated by the inflow of population. Thus the potential mismatch of accommodation size to household demand and the shifts between public and private sector housing have not resulted in abandonment in London, nor have all of the other behavioural problems that appear to affect northern areas been evident.

Government has, however, responded with the declaration of a HMR policy to address the resulting housing issues in specific and designated locations.

2.4 PATHFINDER SCHEME

At the forefront of the initiatives addressing low demand is the HMR pathfinder scheme, a government policy launched in 2003 and designed primarily to improve market conditions in the North of England (ODPM, 2003b; Waters and Karadimitriou, 2006). There are nine pathfinder areas (Figure 2.1), which have been created with £1.2 billion of government funding to deal with the most acute problems and to provide models for successful renewal elsewhere (English Heritage, 2004; Bevan and Dobie, 2006). According to the Audit Commission independent scrutiny, about 700,000 homes are located in the pathfinder areas, including about half of the 1 million properties affected by low demand and abandonment, based on 2002 estimates. The pathfinder areas are to develop a coherent strategy for tackling problems of low housing demand and abandonment as a means of stimulating wider regeneration.

The basic concept associated with the HMR areas is that of improving the existing housing stock, either by refurbishment or by demolition and rebuild (or a combination of both) in those parts of England that have been designated as pathfinder areas and which suffer from low-demand housing (particularly related to an oversupply of pre-1919 terraced homes). The government has addressed this by stating that *"... the economic development of the North is dependent on variety in the housing stock"* (Northern Way Steering Group, 2005: 2).

Bevan and Dobie (2006) have urged the government to set out clear guidance for the pathfinders to follow when deciding which properties to demolish, and to put pressure on the Treasury to ensure that refurbishment is as attractive within the VAT regime as demolition (currently refurbishment is taxed at 17.5% compared with zero rating for new build), although there is no indication that such a change will occur.

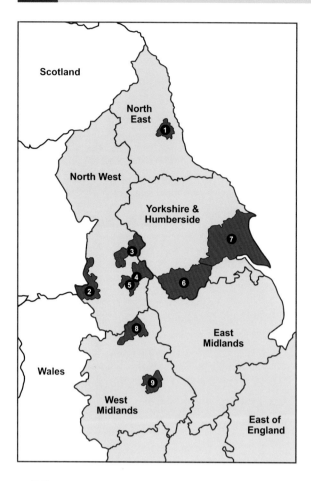

Regions

Local authorities involved in market renewal policy
pathfinders

1   Newcastle, Gateshead

2   Merseyside (Newheartlands)

3   East Lancashire (Elevate)

4   Oldham and Rochdale (Partners in Action)

5   Manchester, Salford

6   South Yorkshire (Transform)

7   Hull and East Riding of Yorkshire

8   North Staffordshire (RENEW)

9   Birmingham and Sandwell

Note: The pathfinder will only cover the parts of
these local authorities most acutely affected
by low demand and abandonment

Figure 2.1: Location of the nine housing market renewal
areas

2.4.1 Case studies: Slater Street, Middleport, and Knutton Village, Staffordshire

Both of these sites are in areas of major intervention within the RENEW North Staffordshire pathfinder project, one of nine such schemes established under the SCP in 2003. The initiative focuses on neighbourhoods in Stoke-on-Trent and Newcastle-under-Lyme. In common with other pathfinders, RENEW aims to tackle a range of issues with a view to upgrading the general condition of housing stock through a mixture of refurbishment and new-build schemes, enhancing the surrounding environment, and coordinating a multi-agency approach to improving the general quality of life for the community through neighbourhood management. Over 2005–2020, RENEW is aiming to invest £2.3 billion to transform the local housing market (RENEW, 2005, 2006a).

The pathfinder is governed by a partnership board comprising representatives of the partner organisations and appointees selected for their knowledge and experience. A paper considered by the partnership board in November 2006 states that:

"Sustainability is probably the key concept that lies at the heart of housing market restructuring. We will only be successful if we make a difference for the long-term and we explicitly build this perspective into all the decisions that we take, and the projects that we decide to fund and/or endorse."
                                              (RENEW, 2006e, p.1)

The board has adopted the BRE EcoHomes framework (see Section 6) for the promotion and delivery of sustainable construction (a minimum of the 'very good' standard for new dwellings, with 'excellent' being sought wherever feasible). It has also endorsed the CABE/HBF 'Building for Life' 'silver' standard for the construction of new dwellings (with the higher 'gold' standard to be sought wherever possible and financially viable), and also the BRE EcoHomes XB rating for the refurbishment of existing private sector dwellings (RENEW, 2006d).

A key mechanism used for evaluating the condition of both building stock and its setting is the neighbourhood renewal assessment (NRA), a process kept under review by CABE and regarded by RENEW as *"a crucial tool in delivering (its) strategic objectives"* (RENEW, 2006c). The NRA is a major influence on decisions about clearance and redevelopment or refurbishment within the framework of the master plan for the area concerned. By giving either a monetary value or a points score to a range of physical, social, economic and environmental indicators, the NRA suggests which of four options – do nothing, repair to a minimum standard, renovate comprehensively, or clear/redevelop – would be the most appropriate (Stoke-on-Trent City Council, 2006).

Both of these case studies are primarily residential areas, with various associated non-residential uses. The Slater Street area consists of 240 Victorian terraced houses in the Middleport neighbourhood of Burslem. It has a history of housing market failure, and was the subject of an NRA carried out in 2005/06. This found that ground conditions were good, but 50% of the property stock was in poor condition, with significant levels of vacancies and conversion from owner-occupation to rented accommodation. A survey of residents undertaken by RENEW in 2006 found the majority to be in favour of clearance and redevelopment, but a subsequent survey organised by the residents themselves discovered that the majority wished for investment to enable them to stay in the area.

A characterisation survey identified that the terraces have a strong identity. A report prepared by GVA Grimley for RENEW and the City Council suggests that current government density targets may be hard to achieve without the acquisition of additional land, which may not be readily available. Given the equivocal view of residents, no further work would be undertaken to progress a compulsory purchase order (CPO) until a master plan had been prepared during the Spring of 2007. In the meantime, RENEW worked with Touchstone Housing Association to acquire properties for improvement, although some owner-occupiers had reportedly been selling up rather than go through a period of further uncertainty (GVA Grimley, 2005; Stoke-on-Trent City Council, 2006; Hope and Sidebottom, 2007).

In contrast to the uncertainty about the future of Slater Street, the strategy for Knutton Village appears more clear cut. Knutton is an industrial village on the north-east edge of Newcastle-under-Lyme, again with a significant quantity of Victorian terraced housing. Even without having to prepare the detailed costings carried out for Slater Street, the NRA undertaken in 2004 and a subsequent structural survey of properties completed in early 2007 indicated that retention of existing stock in the village centre was a feasible option. This will constitute part of a menu of initiatives to be pursued to revitalise the housing market in the Knutton/Cross Heath area as a whole, led partly by RENEW in association with the Borough Council and Aspire Housing Association and partly by the private sector. English Heritage will be commissioning a characterisation survey of the village centre to identify its defining features and suggest how these may be restored (RENEW, 2006b; Hope and Sidebottom, 2007).

Support for this strategy is to be found in the Borough Council's area action plan (AAP) for Knutton and Cross Heath. The sustainability appraisal of the AAP acknowledges local support for raising the profile of the built heritage of the neighbourhood, and states that "it is the intention of the AAP to protect the character of these areas" (Newcastle-under-Lyme Borough Council, 2005: 12).

Given the different approaches to finalising preferred options in these two instances, it might be concluded from evidence in North Staffordshire and the other pathfinder areas such as Liverpool and East Lancashire, where there has been vigorous debate over retention or demolition of existing Victorian terraced housing stock, that where decisions are clear cut (eg due either to poor ground stability or to the extent of physical deterioration), or where evidence from the NRA points strongly to the viability of refurbishment, 'heritage' per se may not be the major determinant. However, it may become a more important consideration where environmental, economic and community factors are more balanced between clearance and refurbishment.

2.4.2 Criticism of the pathfinder programme

The pathfinder scheme has been met with some degree of scepticism, with suggestions that there is a danger that properties in the HMR areas might be demolished and replaced unnecessarily (CPRE, 2004; English Heritage, 2004). Further, as stated by Mumford and Power (cited in Dixon et al., 2005: 59):

"Demolition must be used with care. We found instances where it has triggered further decline and broken up communities …. Local authorities must make clear the purpose of demolition … phased demolition strategies sometimes encouraged stigmatisation and uncertainty."

According to the government's Housing, Planning, Local Government and the Regions Committee (2005: 4) between 2004 and 2006, in the initial stages of the HMR programme, some 10,000 of the targeted Victorian units have been demolished and a further 24,000 refurbishments have been undertaken. It was predicted (*ibid.*) that over 20 years, up to 200,000 homes could be demolished. This has raised concern about the loss of unique examples of Victorian heritage, as well as the waste of resources in adopting a demolition policy.

The concern attached to the demolition policy is in part that the UK's heritage will be lost and in part that the diversity of the housing stock will be threatened, given the proposed large-scale clearances across areas such as Liverpool and Manchester. According to Save Britain's Heritage (SAVE, 2006), between 100,000 and 400,000 pre-1919 terraced homes are under threat of clearance, and the organisation warns against massive clearance programmes, citing the mass clearance of the 1950s and 1960s and the problems that ensued.

There also seems to be concern about the process underpinning the decision to demolish:

"… perfectly decent historic houses are being condemned on the basis of ten minute external surveys in a blatant abuse of the powers granted under the Housing Act. Householders are being forced out of their beloved homes following minimal and misinformed consultations."   (SAVE, undated)

There is also considered to be a conservation element to the debate. According to Bevan and Dobie (2006), the ODPM's HMR initiative is threatening the existence of thousands of houses of great historic value. (This is discussed further in Sections 3 and 4.)

Furthermore, the authors state that all pre-1919 residential properties are at risk of heritage loss, given 'inappropriate' repair and renovation works. According to their work, approximately 20% of the UK housing stock, equating to 4.4 million homes, was built prior to the 1920s: thus vast areas of English heritage are under threat from demolition or poorly managed refurbishments. Intertwined with the physical loss and damage are the elements of cultural and social deprivation, because such traditional buildings are seen to give communities "*a strong local identity, in marked contrast to often soulless modern estates*" (Bevan and Dobie, 2006: 17).

According to the ODPM (2003c), in terms of the built environment, a sustainable community should encompass spaces that are both environmentally sensitive and well designed, and should include a sufficient range, diversity, affordability and accessibility of housing within a balanced housing market. However, while much publicity is given to how to accommodate the predicted growth in households, there is increasing evidence of the growing problem of low demand for housing, which affects around 1 million homes (English Heritage, 2004) in certain locations in the North and Midland areas of England. They can be characterised (Bramley and Pawson, 2002: 397–398) as housing in blocks, estates or management patches, where one or more of the following symptoms is exhibited:

- small or non-existent waiting lists;
- tenancy offers frequently refused;
- high rates of voids available for letting; and
- high rates of tenancy turnover.

Statistics (Bevan and Dobie, 2006: 17) show that the first phase of the pathfinder initiative (which ended in March 2006) involved the demolition of some 10,000 dwellings and the refurbishment of about 24,000. Mass demolition was the preferred policy option in such cases until very recently. The turning of the policy has been an 'urban renaissance', which has brought with it renewed efforts to revive those areas affected by low demand with a strategic approach, combining various measures aiming at re-establishing local communities with self-sustaining private housing markets.

Garlick (2006) states that, because of changes in the local housing markets, there has been a reduction in the scale of the planned demolition within the pathfinder areas. Nonetheless, there are still many areas that are under threat of losing vast numbers of their Victorian terraces.

While it is clear that demolition has its critics, there are significant issues involved in the refurbishment of older residential properties. Sustainability of resources and energy are clearly factors in favour of retaining existing stock, but there is evidence (Bevan and Dobie, 2006) that the professional and artisan skills base is simply inadequate or non-existent to provide sympathetic and appropriate repairs and renewals for a vast number of Victorian and Edwardian buildings. In some locations, for certain property types, the guiding principle of sustainability may therefore mean that demolition is the only option.

Also, in some cases where a building has come to the end of its useful life, or where a structure is seen as a blight on today's communities, it may be preferable to demolish the building, thereby providing new opportunities for a revival in the local housing market. However, in such instances people are likely to be concerned that their local communities will be ruined if these traditional homes are destroyed.

In 2003 CABE produced a document as an 'Agenda for Action' (CABE, 2003), providing guidance for the pathfinder areas based on information and advice from five national organisations (CABE, the Commission for Integrated Transport, English Heritage, the Environment Agency, and the Sustainable Development Commission). The document highlights the most important issues or ambitions to be achieved through housing renewal strategies.

"It seeks to encourage the nine Pathfinders that can spearhead this new approach to regeneration, to raise the debate about our collective responsibility to help them succeed and to inform best practice elsewhere."

(CABE, 2003: 1)

The Agenda for Action provides seven keys for successful HMR:

- realise the scale of the opportunity and the task – by developing an understanding of the causes of, and potential solutions to, market failure from the macro scale (the sub-region) to the micro level (the local community);
- positively address heritage as an asset – by evaluating the existing physical assets of an area and, where possible, enhancing them;
- develop proposals that will create places of distinction and that make sense as a network of settlements;
- recognise the value of good design and its role in regeneration – by placing it at the centre of the initial decision-making process;
- adopt a set of tools and strategies that will help design and deliver high-quality urban environments on the ground;
- place sustainable development at the heart of thinking and action on the urban environment – by designing communities with resource-efficient homes, which encourage sustainable lifestyles; and
- get ready for the challenge – by enhancing capacity and skills within the organisations charged with delivery, providing appropriate support and resources, and targeting some early projects to provide a benchmark for quality.

These seven key actions are developed further in the document, in which issues of community involvement and the community's identification with the 'what' and the 'how' of the plan are reinforced. Also identified is the need for a design 'champion', and the need for:

"... a manageable number of excellent early projects, which if delivered to a high quality, will generate follow-on investment and act as anchors within the renewal area from which other projects can grow." (CABE, 2003: 9)

However, in 2006 it was reported that there had been an apparent government rethink in areas that were formerly designated as demolition sites. According to Early (2006:9), the economic grounds for the policy of demolition of housing were considered weak in some HMR areas. For instance, in Blackburn and Darwen controversy surrounds the assessment of local market housing conditions, which has led to the demolition of existing housing stock, and critics have argued that those responsible have become too hasty and lacklustre in their approach. Housing consultants have felt there has been a lack of attention paid to the market condition in these low-demand areas, and one inspector states that:

"Even if the area was once one of low market demand, there is no compelling evidence that it still is ... The average house price was £20,000 with some as low as £6,000 ... but since the housing market renewal area designation house prices have risen by up to 57% ... Buy to let investment has interfered with the market ... and the people of the community suffer because it costs them more to buy."   (Cited in Early 2006: 9)

2.4.3 Reasons for low-demand areas and abandonment

There are major regional variations in the level and nature of demand and supply for dwellings in the UK. As mentioned above, there are significant amounts of existing housing in locations of low demand, and this causes other social and behavioural problems.

Reviewing the available literature, it is therefore a somewhat complex picture that emerges:

"... low demand is almost always a consequence of economic decline and the demographic changes which result from the loss of local employment. Obsolescent house types and poor physical conditions are also often implicated ... low demand may reflect the relative strength rather than the weakness of the local economy, as affordable homeownership is brought within reach of former tenants gaining a foothold in a growing labour market."   (Bramley and Pawson, 2002: 419)

Bramley and Pawson (2002: 396) suspect that the phenomenon of low demand and abandonment has in part resulted from *"the exhaustion of various adjustment mechanisms"* and also the fact that previously attempted solutions will no longer work. For example, the 1960s policy of shifting work to areas of low employment in the English regions is no longer appropriate in a global economy (p. 408).

Bramley and Pawson (2002: 410) identify potentially relevant public policies that might form part of the solution, including public order initiatives and the land use planning system. However, with a failure of public authorities to recognise the problem fully, partly because of a fear of loss of government funding, current policies are not providing potential solutions. However, other research suggests that:

"Housing abandonment is the end product of a complex interaction between national and local factors. Far too little is known about the economic context, the policy processes at work locally and nationally and very little indeed is known about the complex sociology of traumatised neighbourhoods which spiral downward ... The relationship between low demand and abandonment also needs further clarification ..."
                         (Keenan et al., 1999: 715)

There is also the existence of ageing stock (Table 2.1), some of which has not been refurbished to what might be termed a sustainable standard. Yet, of itself, poor-quality housing cannot be the sole cause of low demand and abandonment, given the fact that such conditions are limited to certain locations, and that the high percentages of pre-1919 dwellings are not limited to those areas.

To achieve a sustainable standard in the existing housing stock would involve a major national programme of improvement, probably necessitating a 1960s-style grant aid programme, alongside a public awareness campaign. There is evidence that even if there was discernible demand for eco-refurbishment, the supply side simply could not respond because of significant failures in the construction industry, as discussed later in this report.

Yet, given the scale of the problem, the unsustainable nature of the current UK demolition and construction processes, the sheer costs involved, and the social and environmental implications, the challenge for the pathfinder areas cannot be avoided. If these pathfinder areas can be successfully regenerated by housing-led initiatives, then, as CABE (2003) indicated above, other investments and projects will follow.

Table 2.1: Age structure of UK housing stock

Region	Percentage of dwellings							All dwellings ('000s)
	Pre-1851	1851 to 1918	1919 to 1945	1946 to 1964	1965 to 1984	1985 to 1994	Post-1994	
North East	1	14	19	25	25	7	9	1,126
North West	3	19	21	20	23	7	6	2,989
Yorkshire and Humber	5	14	20	21	25	8	7	2,190
East Midlands	5	12	15	22	30	10	6	1,843
West Midlands	4	9	19	29	27	7	5	2,259
East	4	10	15	24	31	10	6	2,361
London	2	25	31	17	17	4	4	3,146
South East	4	13	15	22	30	9	6	3,466
South West	8	15	13	20	28	10	6	2,236
England	4	15	19	22	26	8	6	21,613

It is the opportunity to create new and modern spaces that has encouraged some local authorities to opt for demolition plans, where market failure, abandonment and secondary problems such as anti-social behaviour have created a multitude of problems for local communities. The main argument for this is that the housing stock in these areas has become unattractive to owners and potential owners, and those people who can afford to move out have done so. This has left a sporadic population, in some instances with failing infrastructure and a lack of services. An example where demolition was considered the most suitable solution to restructuring a local housing market is shown in the case example in Case study 1.

The debate in the Darwen example (see Case study 1) focused on the choice of whether to demolish and rebuild, or to refurbish. These choices are discussed further in later sections of the report. However, the concept of sustainable construction needs to be presented in the light of the pathfinder initiative.

Case study 1: Case example – proposed demolition of housing in Darwen

Darwen Borough Council sought to demolish 152 Victorian terraced homes located in the East Lancashire pathfinder area in order to address its problem of low demand.

According to Early (2006), over 90% of the homes were acquired through voluntary agreements and the majority of the homes have been demolished on the grounds that property prices over the previous years had reflected it as an area of low demand.

Early (2006) reported that the average house price was £20,000, with some as low as £6,000 prior to demolition. The local authority maintained that demolishing housing in some parts was the correct decision in housing quality terms.

2.5 AGENDA FOR SUSTAINABLE CONSTRUCTION

In terms of residential development in the UK, the government's sustainable development agenda is based on the concept of meeting four concurrent objectives (DETR, 2000a):

- social progress that meets the needs of everyone;
- effective protection of the environment;
- prudent use of natural resources; and
- maintenance of high and stable levels of economic growth and employment.

The DTI publication *Building a Better Quality of Life: A strategy for more sustainable construction* (DTI, 2000: 5) established key themes for action by the construction industry. These include:

- designing for minimum waste;
- lean construction;
- minimising energy in construction and use;
- respecting people and the local environment; and
- monitoring and reporting (ie the use of benchmarks).

The government has attempted to direct the sustainable construction and environmental standard of residential property through the planning system and, more recently, by the introduction of sustainable building codes, working alongside existing EcoHomes ratings (for more on this see Section 6.3). The Code for Sustainable Homes, launched in 2005, seeks to rate the environmental performance of buildings on a one to six star scale (with the highest rating representing 'carbon neutral')(DCLG, 2005).

The Royal Institution of Chartered Surveyors (RICS), in its response to the Department of Trade and Industry's UK Energy Review, felt that a more prescriptive form of assessing environmentally sound buildings, together with quantifiable indicators, was required (RICS, 2006). This debate would suggest that a greater level of certainty is required in decision-making processes when assessing individual sites for development potential and, more importantly, when considering the options for retention of existing stock or the prospects for its replacement with new-build development. It seems clear that either option requires an appreciation of innovative sustainable construction and day-to-day operational efficiency in order to meet the objectives of sustainable development.

Regional development agencies act as key drivers at a strategic level, coordinating economic development across the UK regions. They are well positioned to drive and lead innovation in the construction sector. The planning framework sets out an overarching policy, and has a role in guiding and monitor the implementation of sustainable development.

A collection of sustainable construction initiatives has been introduced, which has been designed to improve knowledge transfer and practice. The Egan review (2004), a government-commissioned analysis, sought to review the skills and training of the UK construction industry to deliver sustainable communities. The report which highlighted the lack of skills also sought to promote a sustainable communities code of practice that would give clear information and guidance about environmental standards, thereby providing incentives for achieving long-term aims, such as reducing carbon emissions and minimising waste. The report recommended that the local development framework should be the key driving mechanism.

In support of Egan's findings, the Sustainable Buildings Task Group was established in 2003 to identify cost-effective improvements in quality and the environmental performance of buildings. The Task Group asked that:

- a single national code for sustainable buildings should be established, incorporating existing measures such as BREEAM;
- existing Building Regulations should be extended to give broader sustainability considerations; and
- sustainability in the construction industry should be encouraged through improved training (Sustainable Building Task Group, 2004).

2.5.1 Drivers for sustainable construction

According to the DTI (2006), there is a wide range of factors that are encouraging developers to adopt sustainable practices:

- Sustainable development is a core objective of UK and European government policy with the requirement that national CO_2 emissions be cut by 20% by 2010 (based on 1990 levels).
- Sustainability is central to UK planning policy (eg PPS1, PPS22).
- It is a legal requirement that sustainability appraisals be undertaken as part of regional and local planning policy.
- The landfill tax, aggregates levy, climate change levy, and stamp duty exemption for deprived areas have all been introduced to provide economic incentives.
- Development agencies are tasked with promoting sustainable development, and are building such requirements into procurement processes, for example requirements to meet EcoHomes or BREEAM rating targets.
- Forthcoming legislation, including the Energy Performance of Buildings Directive, updates to Part L of the Building Regulations, and the implementation of the Sustainable and Secure Buildings Act, is designed to increase minimum standards relating to sustainable construction.

However, the construction industry is notoriously traditional in its practices, and there is evidence that most companies have made no or only limited steps towards sustainable solutions. The reasons for this include continuing problems reaching small and medium-sized enterprises, the supply chain (as shown later in this report), insufficient awareness within the construction professions and trades, and the confusing nature of the sheer volume of information and initiatives is confusing (Sustainable Construction Task Group, 2003: 6; see also van Bueren and Priemus, 2002).

Anon (2005: 1) reports the results of a study by Wates Group (building contractors) thus:

"Most of the major construction programmes designed to create 'sustainable communities' are pre-programmed to fail ... [because] real life procurement and construction industry practices are not matching the rhetoric. This will continue until such time as policy makers translate theories into hard practical actions at procurer and construction company level and measure and reward best practice."

The report (*ibid.*) argues that because the parties in the procurement, design, build and maintenance processes are not rewarded on the basis of measures of a development's whole life financial and environmental cost, the following will continue:

- procurement authorities and the construction industry have no single set of easy-to-follow financial, environmental and social performance measures, based on whole life costings;
- there will be a failure to establish and police such measures;
- most non-PFI public sector construction programmes will continue to be driven by the need to keep short-term costs low;
- flexible buildings will not be achieved until the construction industry actions such things as better soundproofing and easy-to-maintain materials; and
- performance measures will not itemise the practical key components of a sustainable development across the supply chain.

The Wates study (*ibid.*) argues that government intervention is required in the form of tax incentives to drive improvements in waste management, water harvesting and reductions in CO_2 emissions, and also calls for amendments to EU legislation to accommodate the social benefits of using local suppliers on long-term development programmes.

2.6 IMPROVING ENVIRONMENTAL SUSTAINABILITY OF HOUSING STOCK

National government, through its climate change strategy, aims to reduce UK carbon emissions by 20% by 2010 (over 1990 levels), and recognises that the residential sector has a large part to play in the development of the UK sustainable agenda. McEvoy *et al.* 1999 state that one third of CO_2 produced in the UK comes from residential property (both construction and occupation), and it is anticipated that up to 25% of these emissions could be saved cost-effectively (Department of the Environment, 1997).

Clearly, substantial improvements in residential energy efficiency are required if the UK is to meet its target for reduced carbon emissions (Jones and Leach, 2000). However, the debate now concerns whether changes in policy activity is sufficient to bring about the needed change (Jones *et al.*, 2001).

In October 2006 the UK government called for a radical reform in the house Building Regulations in an effort to cut national CO_2 emission trends in accordance with the latest climate change strategy. Housing Minister Yvette Cooper said that work still needed to be done on the affordability and environmental performance of the UK housing stock, and that this represents a major challenge for the industry.

2.7 SUMMARY

There is clear evidence of a desire from the government and from interested national organisations (such as CABE, English Heritage and the RICS) that the problems of the pathfinder areas should be resolved, at least initially, in the provision of suitable quality and quantity of housing for the needs of the local markets.

More than the nature and quality of the built environment is at stake here. There are clear indications that negative social and economic consequences follow from – or cause – the existence of areas of low housing demand and total abandonment. It seems that the solutions of the past (large-scale demolition and rebuild, coupled with employment-based incentives) are no longer appropriate.

Given that the pathfinder areas have been designated, that funding has been obtained, and that their programmes have been in place for some time, it is possible to evaluate and comment on their success (or otherwise); and critics have focused specifically on the choice available to those responsible for the pathfinder policies of either demolishing and rebuilding the rejected housing stock, or refurbishing it to an appropriate standard. There are a range of issues underpinning the making of such a choice, including sustainability awareness and incentives, the skills and commitment of the construction industry, and also, to some extent, community awareness. However, in the longer term, the loss of (what some argue to be) heritage buildings, and issues of reflecting not merely initial costs but also occupational costs or costs in use, need to be considered.

3 DEMOLITION AND NEW BUILD

3.1 INTRODUCTION

Demolition and new build is an attractive, neat and flexible choice for pathfinder areas. It allows for a sweeping away of the old (structures, services, designs and layouts) and replacement with new, modern accommodation, which has the opportunity to reflect all of the criteria that the government seeks to meet within its sustainable communities programme, not merely in the individual properties, but also in the wider community.

Of course, some dwellings may well have come to the end of their useful lives, and for reasons of poor-quality structures and services demolition may be the only option. However, it is an expensive solution, in terms of financial, environmental and social costs.

Design and new build was a policy widely used in the 1960s and 1970s. It was intensely criticised for its destruction of communities that (apparently) functioned well (and which could therefore be regarded today as sustainable), and also for the quality (or lack of quality) of the dwellings that were developed subsequently. As a solution it is therefore unlikely to find favour with those members of the public who remember the outcome of that policy, and who fear that such pathfinder outcomes:

"… will repeat the mistakes of previous clearance programmes that destroyed the heritage of areas and failed to replace it with neighbourhoods of lasting value"
(Bevan and Dobie, 2006: 17).

3.2 DEMOLITION

There has been great pressure for additional clearance of low-demand residential areas in the last 30 years, expressed most recently through the HMR pathfinder scheme. According to the ODPM statistics (Kintrea and Morgan, 2005), 'slum' clearance peaked in the 1960s, and the diminishing trend in the volume of clearance is attributable to a variety of factors:

- mass clearance in the 1960s and 1970s meant that the 'very worst' pre-1919 housing was demolished. The support for continued clearance became less powerful because of economic reasoning and community opposition;
- community opposition peaked, with pressure groups asking for British heritage to be saved. The programmes of the 1960s were stereotyped as

the dismantling of local communities, and people became dissatisfied with Victorian terraced housing being replaced with, for instance, high-rise public housing; and
- there was a general shift towards housing stock improvements, with resources switching from clearance and redevelopment to renewal. With the introduction of general improvement areas and housing action areas during the 1970s, political priorities began to change.

The major challenge represented by the HMR scheme is to match the private sector improvements of the 1970s and 1980s, which saw the creation of sustainable neighbourhoods in areas of more robust housing need, such as London. However, areas of low demand, particularly those in northern England, are suffering, in part as a consequence of poor standards of accommodation. This has left local authorities debating how best to deal with the problem – whether to improve the standard of existing residential units, or undertake site clearance, with or without new build.

This is an important point. Given that there is low demand, there seems little point in rebuilding accommodation that no one wants (or, at least, which no one within the locality wants). A policy of demolition without rebuild allows for the creation of other resources, such as open spaces, community facilities, and these opportunities could greatly enhance the success of the demolition and rebuild policy and the restructuring of the local housing market.

English Heritage recognises that there may be a need to reduce the number of existing dwellings *"where it has been shown to be the way forward following a thorough and transparent analysis at a sub-regional and neighbourhood level"* (English Heritage, 2005: 1). But English Heritage states (*ibid.*) that clearance will be more appropriate in areas of poor-quality spaces and housing layouts, with problems of oversupply, choice and housing mix.

Bramley and Pawson (2002: 418) state that levels of clearance of private sector housing have been very low for a number of years, which reflects *"the policy presumptions"* resulting from the mass clearances of the 1970s, together with a perception, within the private sector at least, that compulsory purchase and clearance are fraught with practical, political, financial and procedural difficulties. The authors comment on the then DETR's perceptions that local authorities have limited experience and therefore a poor understanding of how to make the complex and time-consuming CPO procedures work. Local authorities themselves regard their present powers as inadequate, and there is growing nervousness about the implications of the EU Human Rights Act for this and other aspects of planning (*ibid.*).

Demolition of private housing stock is recognised (*ibid.*: 418) as an expensive option, which will include compensation at levels that *"often look suspiciously higher than market value"*, and may also be higher because of the 'pepperpotting' spread of those properties earmarked for clearance, and the need to support the ends of the remaining terraced stock. Bramley and Pawson (2002) estimate that increasing private sector demolitions by a factor of 10 (from 2,000 to 20,000 per year) might deal with half of the currently estimated low-demand private sector stock in 10 years, at a cost of around £5 billion. This is a major financial commitment, and one that should be unacceptable in a country with a recognised and severe chronic housing shortage.

However, there are major sustainability issues and, in particular, energy wastage/conservation issues associated with a policy of widespread demolition. Bramley and Pawson (2002) highlight the environmental considerations involved, given the huge investment in terms of embodied energy (represented by the existing housing stock):

"… demolition and replacement means not only the loss of embodied energy in the old buildings and expending energy in demolition, but the generation of further carbon emissions in the materials and building processes of the new properties." (ibid.: 18)

However, in some cases, the energy used in demolition and replacement may be lower than the energy wasted over time in the refurbishment and continued occupation of an older building with lower levels of insulation etc, although the view is expressed that *"traditional buildings do not waste energy if they are properly maintained"* (Bramley and Pawson, 2002: 18). Thus it is not enough merely to compare the costs (economic and energy) at the point of demolition and rebuild or refurbishment. A longer-term view, which also reflects the costs in use of a building during its entire future useful life, needs to be taken into account (see Section 6).

At a local level, however, it seems there is a presumption in favour of demolition, fuelled by pressure from developers to build/sell new homes, and from local authorities and housing associations, which are attracted by the opportunity to exchange older houses in need of repair for new-build ones that can be cheaper to maintain and may provide a greater rental return. Nevertheless, there is evidence that an attractive urban environment can be achieved by refurbishment of existing buildings.

"Much praised projects … require a great deal more thought and planning than simply clearing an empty space for a developer to move in. Innovative developments that conserve an area's heritage therefore involve a commitment of much greater resources by both planning departments and developers." (Bevan and Dobie, 2006: 19)

The principal drawback to this approach to redevelopment is that both the demolition and the construction of buildings produce an enormous amount of waste, and, as described below, result in a significant proportion of the total waste stream. However, disposal for demolition waste is more cost-effective, in terms both of building costs and of time. Specifically, there are protracted handling procedures for materials common in pre-1970 residential units, for instance in relation to lead-based and asbestos-based materials. Of greatest concern, however, is the lack of provision made in new build for future disassembly and reuse of materials (Chini and Bruening, 2003: 2), which merely means that similar problems will face future generations unless the construction industry takes on board both the policy and the practice of building to reuse.

3.3 WASTE FROM DEMOLITION

According to the DETR (2000b: 11), 70 million tonnes of waste are removed from construction and demolition sites and taken to landfill each year. At the same time, landfill tax costs are increasing: they are predicted to rise from £3 per tonne to £10 per tonne in 2010. Clearly, better management is required. Carter (2006) explains that approximately £150 million can be saved by investing in innovative waste management strategies, such as the increased uptake of on-site recycling. Assessment tools, such as BRE SMARTwaste and the National Green Specification's WasteCost Calculator, are likely to improve this process. The demolition of building structures produces an exceptional amount of material, which in many countries results in a significant waste stream.

Demolition waste from the construction and demolition (C&D) industry in the USA amounts to 136 million tonnes annually, of which more than 90% is dumped in landfill sites. In contrast, in the Netherlands C&D waste amounts to 15 million tonnes per year and, through a greater environmental awareness and strict government legislation, over 80% of this waste stream is recycled.

While government legislation in the Netherlands prohibits the dumping of reusable waste, the Technical University Delft (Kilber and Chini, 2000) found that reusing components of existing buildings is not always easy or cheap. For instance, recovered components such as bricks are costly to remove, and the techniques of complete reuse or deconstruction are not wholly competitive with new products. Research by the Deutsch-Französisches Institut für Umweltforschung (*ibid.*) found that the waste stream in Germany is estimated to be approximately 45 million tonnes per year, of which 25% is concrete and 50% is bricks and stone.

In terms of construction and demolition waste in the UK, 53 million tonnes are produced annually and, according to research undertaken by BRE and the Universities of Sheffield and Salford (Kilbert and Chini, 2000), just under half of this waste is being recycled. These authors highlight the difficulties resulting from the fact that large proportions of mixed waste (both inert and active waste combined) are generated by the construction industry, and that this category is subject to a significantly higher landfill tax rate (£10 per tonne) than separated waste, which incurs landfill rates of only £2 per tonne.

It is clear from these examples that if more careful separation and reuse/recycling of materials were standard practice, or if deconstruction was a standardised process, reclamation of materials would increase, costs of demolition would decrease, and there would be many potential benefits for the construction and property sector as well as the second-hand market in salvaged materials.

However, for reasons of embodied energy and community stability, and despite the potential for salvage and reclamation, demolition should, on balance, be a last resort. Therefore:

"Developers and planners must be persuaded to consider all alternatives before they opt for demolition, and those charged with caring for older buildings must ensure that they understand how they function."

(Bevan and Dobie, 2006: 20)

The high level of waste resulting from demolition of existing buildings could be greatly reduced if buildings were to be constructed in such a way that their component parts that are capable of reuse when the building itself no longer has a useful life could be easily removed and reused, ie deconstruction (Chini and Bruening, 2003). Deconstruction requires designing buildings in such a way that dismantling (rather than demolition) of the component parts of the structure is both technically and economically feasible. Such a technique involves more than just a reuse of specific historical/architectural features made available through salvage operations. It also covers the provision of a range of reuse and recycling opportunities for such components as slates, bricks and roof timbers, and has major implications for the way new buildings are designed and constructed. According to the research, when a building reaches the end of its useful life, renovating the structure for reuse is always preferable to demolition.

This is, of course, a solution for the future, but one that needs careful consideration and early implementation if we are not to be dealing with similar problems of waste in the next century. Chini and Bruening (2003) acknowledge the fact that refurbishment and deconstruction (involving the reclamation of materials) is, by its very nature, a relatively lengthy and labour-intensive process. However, the reduction in waste (see Section 3.3) and the retention of embodied energy are highly significant, as is the impact on the need for new materials in any refurbishment or reuse programme.

3.4　SUMMARY

The perceived failure of mass clearance policies in the past, admittedly also associated with the failure of the dwellings that were built as replacements, fuels a widespread prejudice against demolition as a solution to low-demand housing.

Demolition as a process destroys the embodied energy in existing buildings and, together with the anticipated and ensuing rebuilding process, generates vast quantities of waste. Previous experience of demolition and rebuild also indicates that such replacement dwellings will have a shorter useful life than the dwellings that they replace.

There are situations where demolition and rebuild may be the only option – where the fabric, structure, services etc of dwellings are either entirely unsuitable for refurbishment, or where the costs are very high. Where the layout of the dwellings and their immediate surroundings is incapable of adaptation to make it attractive to current potential owners or occupiers, again, demolition might be appropriate.

Given the previous UK experience, it is increasingly difficult to justify a policy of demolition and rebuild, although if a solution could be found to the issue of construction and demolition waste, and to allay the suspicion that replacement dwellings will not be as sustainable as the original, then it might be easier to change public perceptions.

4 REFURBISHMENT

4.1 INTRODUCTION

Over recent years the rehabilitation and reuse of old buildings (often for new uses) have become an increasingly attractive and viable alternative to demolition and redevelopment. There are many reasons for this trend, both for individual buildings and for larger areas. To some extent, refurbishment can be seen as a reaction to the much-criticised policies of mass clearance and new build of the 1960s and 1970s (see Section 3).

However, other reasons can be identified for the preference for refurbishment rather than demolition. First, there is the question of image – the perception that new buildings can in no way replicate the structural and unique architectural qualities of the old. Second, there may be planning and legislative constraints, which currently favour retention rather than clearance, especially in inner city sites. Thirdly, and perhaps most importantly, there is the influence of economic and financial criteria.

Generally speaking, older buildings, because of their age and structural condition, could be acquired relatively cheaply. Increasingly, developers and end-users are seeing that value can be attached to old and often heritage buildings, and that the retention of historic or architecturally important buildings has a monetary value as well as environmental and social benefits. It is also recognised that preservation of historic buildings is best secured by ensuring their continued economic use.

Buildings are continually becoming obsolete for the purpose for which they were originally intended, particularly with the revolutionary changes in the manufacturing industry sector over the past century and more recently with technological innovations. This has resulted in a large stock of such buildings coming onto the market, many of them worthy of retention through rehabilitation and a change of use.

In addition to a growing number of former mills, factories and warehouses in several of the country's 19th-century industrial towns, there are numerous obsolete institutional buildings, schools, hospitals, civic premises and office blocks for which new purposes are being found. There are many examples of successful rehabilitation and conversion of these inner city buildings for residential use, and some of the most innovative developers, such as Urban Splash, are making profits from redevelopment opportunities as a core business activity.

Table 4.1 lists the main advantages of retention and rehabilitation of old buildings compared with demolition and rebuild.

Existing construction (design and materials) and the state of repair have a significant influence on the costs of conversion. For instance, ceiling heights may not be adequate for modern-day use, and timber construction may need modernising for compliance with modern Building Regulations. Therefore an important prerequisite to any decision made as to whether to rehabilitate or rebuild is the preparation of a detailed cost feasibility analysis.

Table 4.1: **The main advantages of retention and rehabilitation of old buildings compared with demolition**

Shorter timescales	The work involved in rehabilitation is normally much less than that needed for demolition, site clearance and construction of new buildings, provided major structural and infrastructural changes are not necessary. There are time savings, too, at the pre-contract design and planning stages.
Financial benefits	These benefits have been categorised by the shorter contract duration, which reduces the effects of inflation on building costs; and the shorter development period, which reduces the cost of providing finance for the scheme and allows the client to obtain the building sooner, therefore beginning to earn revenue from it (for example, rentals or gains occupation) at an earlier date.
Environmental benefits	Most schemes of rehabilitation are justified on the grounds of the architectural or historic qualities of the buildings and of their impact on their immediate environment. In many respects such buildings represent an irreplaceable stock in terms of design and character. Regardless of the architecture or other physical qualities of the building, refurbishment is significantly less intrusive and disruptive of environmental, social and community fabric.

4.2   CONSERVATION-LED REGENERATION

Most of the legal powers for the retention of England's heritage are defined under the Planning (Listed Buildings and Conservation Areas) Act 1990, supplemented by PPG15 and PPG16. However, a major barrier to the conservation of listed buildings is the need to find a contemporary use for them. An additional issue for local planning authorities is the lack of relevant skills and qualified staff, with approximately one quarter of planning authorities having no staff in the conservation field (Cullingworth and Nadin, 2006). There are also indications of a limited skills base within the construction industry for achieving appropriate and sympathetic refurbishment of heritage buildings (English Heritage, 2003: 74).

English Heritage (2004 and 2003) presents its case for conservation-led regeneration based on the following points:

- Houses are among our most important historic assets.
- The range and variability of terraced housing types and their relationship to the landscape often provide a strong local identity.
- Most terraced housing continues to be popular and sufficiently flexible for modern living. It is also recognised that "the conversion of other redundant historic buildings … can also be hugely successful in building confidence and acting as a catalyst for further regeneration" (English Heritage, 2004: 1).
- The adaptation and reuse of historic buildings is environmentally sustainable – representing, as it does, "a huge investment in embodied environment". English Heritage (2003) estimates that the cost of repairing a typical Victorian terraced house is between 40% and 60% less than replacing it with a new build.
- Repair and refurbishment is cost-effective, because much of the historic housing is robust and highly adaptable "and, with regular maintenance could survive almost indefinitely" (English Heritage, 2004: 1). Also, older housing costs less to maintain and occupy over the long-term life of the dwelling than more modern housing (English Heritage, 2003).

While English Heritage recognises the need for demolition under certain circumstances, it stresses that places of real value with the potential for imaginative renewal should not be swept away, and that decisions should be based on an informed understanding of the wider historic environment.

"The enduring success of many traditional high density settlement patterns suggests they might act as a useful model for new development."   (English Heritage, 2004: 1)

However, as mentioned earlier, refurbishment must be appropriate to achieve all the stated aims: "*Inappropriate repair and renovation work actually causes more harm than good*" (Bevan and Dobie, 2006: 17). The problem, it seems (*ibid.*: 19–20), is that "*UK builders and surveyors have lost sight of the principles and techniques used by the Victorians*", and, as a result, where Victorian houses are renovated, the application of 21st-century techniques may destroy the integrity of the original structure and build up trouble for the future.

Recognising that the traditional technologies are rapidly dying out, and that the traditional skills base is in short supply, the National Heritage Training Group is seeking to address the shortage of traditional craft skills, as are the RICS and the Society for the Protection of Ancient Buildings (SPAB), which are seeking to improve the level of understanding of older buildings among built environment professionals.

As English Heritage (2003) points out, the wider, historic environment has an important role to play in realising the ambitions of reuse and renewal on brownfield sites in urban localities. This is especially true of housing (eg Victorian or Edwardian terraced housing, some of which may be back-to-back) in the new pathfinder areas, affecting 1 million homes spread across 120 local authorities in the North and Midlands.

English Heritage (English Heritage, 2004: 1) states that "*where the historic housing is distinctive, retains its coherence and is valued by the local community, English Heritage will favour an approach which promotes its repair and refurbishment as an alternative to new build.*"

4.3   HERITAGE AND REGENERATION

The title of the (then) ODPM's Sustainable Communities initiative, launched in 2003, indicates that sustainability is as much to do with development and support of communities as it is to do with the production and management of the built assets upon which these communities depend. The heritage value ascribed to the built environment may be obvious, to the extent that it is protected in some way by legislation. Equally, however, such value may be more subtle and more personal; it may have evolved over a long period of time, and may have different meanings to different people (Orbasli, 2007).

Despite the contemporary emphasis on sustainability in development of the built environment, the concept is not a new one. Certainly, in the early 1970s, the architect Alex Gordon was championing "*long life, low energy, loose fit*" buildings as a means of providing maximum potential flexibility in use as circumstances changed over time without the need to demolish the structure (Gordon, 1974).

There is a measure of agreement in the literature that heritage forms an important focus in regeneration schemes – although it should be noted that, despite the rich seam of literature on the general purpose and scope of urban regeneration, a definition of heritage-led regeneration is more elusive. However, a range of sources such as Tiesdell *et al.* (1996), English Heritage (1998), SAVE (1998), Pickard and de Thyse (2001) and Beecham (2002) have all pointed to the important contribution that conservation can make to regeneration.

For example, SAVE (1998: 7) argues that *"the historic environment helps make places legible by rooting them in a historic context. It helps inform communities about who they are and where they are. It gives them a sense of identity"*. English Heritage (1998: 4) suggests that *"conservation can provide the catalyst for the sustainable regeneration of whole areas by adopting familiar and cherished old buildings to new uses"*, a philosophy also embraced by the Prince's Regeneration Trust through its fostering of the Regeneration Through Heritage (RTH) initiative, set up in 1996 to support partnerships in revitalising vacant or underused historic buildings. *"RTH promotes the re-use of heritage industrial buildings at risk, principally by assisting community partnerships to develop project proposals for particular buildings"* (PRT, undated: 1).

More recently, the Heritage Lottery Fund (HLF), the Department for Culture, Media and Sport (DCMS) and CABE have all expressed similar views.

"Regeneration involves transforming places that have suffered economic, social or environmental decline. Heritage is often at the heart of those places, whether in the form of a decaying local landmark, boarded up historic buildings or a neglected Victorian park that has become unsafe and unloved. Shared memories may have been lost as communities have fragmented through isolation or poverty."
(Heritage Lottery Fund, 2004: 3)

The Heritage Lottery Fund (2004) takes a broad and populist (as opposed to elitist) view of heritage and promotes heritage conservation as an integral part of urban and rural regeneration, because of the economic, social and environmental benefits that accrue.

CABE (2003) argues for such factors as physical quality, including design and fitness for purpose, but also the length of the building's usable life, to be taken into consideration before the building needs to be replaced. Versatility of design is mentioned as important for possible reuse, as is the quality of the materials used in construction.

4.4 HERITAGE AND PATHFINDER SCHEMES

Pathfinder schemes have been controversial in recent years. Nelson in Lancashire is an area where there were proposals to demolish substantial areas of 19th-century terraced housing, but this was overturned at public inquiry in 2002 (Yates, 2006). Heritage Link (2004) noted that:

"A key argument that local people put to the public inquiry was that it is cheaper to maintain older houses than to build new ones. Why, they asked, spend £80k on new buildings when it only costs £25k to bring existing houses up to modern standards? In terms of sustainability you could not look for a more common sense solution."

One remark by English Heritage that is often quoted is that *"to demolish a Victorian terraced house is to throw away enough embodied energy to drive a car around the world five times. None of this is wasted if the building is refurbished."* Such a comment is a very vivid indication of the loss of energy involved in demolition, and has an emotive effect, but the claim has not been substantiated. DCMS and DTLR (2001: 45) make the same argument: *"What is clear is that, in many cases, far from obstructing change, the remains of the past can act as a powerful catalyst for renewal and a stimulus to high-quality new design and development."*

Graham *et al.* (2000: 168 *et seq.*) consider that there are three particular roles that (what they refer to as) *"the heritage of the conserved built environment, and culture more widely"* play in urban regeneration:

Cachet
The inclusion of heritage buildings, areas and their associated products, events and experiences, which can inject an aura of respectability, continuity and patronage into a more wide-ranging programme containing features that might appear prosaic in comparison. Restoration and reuse of key buildings in the area can inject an element of confidence. The Prince's Regeneration Trust website and other sources such as URBED and the Department of the Environment (1987), Haskell (1993), SAVE (1998) and English Heritage (1998) contain a range of examples of this kind of project.

Animation
The liveliness and activity generated by people being encouraged back onto the streets through their places of residence or employment in a hitherto rundown area.

Externalities
The wider impacts that can flow from an area becoming associated with some kind of environmental improvement or cultural attraction, even if these are of marginal economic viability in themselves.

In *Power of Place*, the review of the historic environment that it coordinated at the request of the government, English Heritage (2000) made a case for the wider economic benefits of using the historic environment as a foundation for regeneration. These arguments were based on the evidence (*ibid.*: Section 16) that, on average, £10,000 of English Heritage grant levered in £48,000 of matching funding from other public and private sector sources. Such a level of English Heritage spending also helped deliver 177 m² of improved commercial floor space, two new or safeguarded jobs and a new home, as well as securing improvements to the historic environment.

Similarly, conservation-led regeneration has encouraged private sector investment, both by retaining businesses in a locality and by providing an incentive to attract such investment into the area. English Heritage (*ibid.*: Section 17) argues that this policy of putting resources into a neighbourhood because of the value of what is already there, rather than labelling it as 'deprived', builds community and business confidence, as do works to improve the maintenance of the public areas, including streets, public parks and gardens.

English Heritage considers that most historic buildings are fully capable of economic use. Despite the restrictions imposed by legislation, it argues that listing often adds to the value of private houses, despite the extra responsibilities.

"In 1998 the investment return on listed office property was 11.9%, compared with 11.4% for unlisted property. Over 18 years, listed and unlisted office property has achieved near-identical returns (8.8% as against 8.9%). The intangible value of using well-loved buildings which add character to an area is difficult to measure, but is recognised by businesses that give high priority to employee and customer satisfaction."

(English Heritage, 2000: Section 18)

It is well recognised within the heritage industry that existing buildings embody historic environment capital – *"the bricks have been fired, the aggregates won, the timber felled, and energy and effort have gone into the process of design and construction"* (English Heritage, 2000: Section 23). So, even where new buildings can be shown to be more energy efficient than existing buildings (which is not always the case), the non-renewable resources involved in the process of demolition and rebuilding are energy-consuming in themselves.

It is clear, however, that the effective reuse of existing fabric will not always be market led. There are pressures for new build, which may in the short term be perceived as easier and cheaper – particularly if only initial costs (rather than costs in use over the future useful life of the building) are compared. Recognising this, English Heritage (2000: Section 24) states that *"intervention may be needed to ensure that external long-term costs and benefits are taken into account"* (see Section 6).

Drivers Jonas (2006) repeats many of the arguments above, when it advises developers of the need to achieve practical outcomes from sustainable development, and to ensure that such development is relevant to the public and engages its interest. It also reminds them that sustainable outcomes (including the reduction of greenhouse gas emissions and the reduction of landfill waste) can be achieved from reusing historic buildings,

Finally, Hunt (2004) has argued that what he calls *"Britain's most forward-looking Victorian cities"*, such as Birmingham, Manchester and Liverpool, have used their 19th-century legacy as the catalyst for regeneration strategies rather than promote further demolition. In order to succeed further, local authorities had to be given greater independence to decide priorities, instead of such decisions being appropriated by central government (Ezard, 2004; Hunt, 2004). However, Larkham (1996: 13–15) summarises a range of arguments against the casual use of the term 'heritage' as an all-embracing marketing concept. However, Larkam

(*ibid.*: 15) observes that *"heritage conservation must be selective, or there would be little change in urban structures, which would then ossify: some change is a necessity."*

There is a link between affordable housing and sustainability. It is argued by the Empty Homes Agency in the UK that it is much more economic to refurbish an existing building than to build new (Ireland, 2005). Similar arguments are advanced in the United States. Rypkema (2002) makes the case for older buildings to be refurbished for affordable housing, quoting the New York experience:

"Common Ground's effort to restore old New York City buildings – preferably historic landmarks – to their former splendour and then place them into the care of homeless or low-income individuals seemed like a "far-fetched vision" in the early 1990s when the nonprofit started out. Four projects later, and more on the way, its innovative approach has not only proven to be a success, it shows the path to cost-effective supportive affordable housing in the city and elsewhere."

(Rypkema, 2002: 17)

There is another aspect of affordable housing in addition to considerations of sustainability: historic buildings tend to be in the centre of town and cities. The consequences of this are that travel distance is reduced and that more journeys are walkable, both of which will reduce the consumption of energy. Rypkema (2002: 7–8) offers the following statistics:

- "Over 40% of residents on older and historic neighbourhoods are within five miles of work. Less than one resident in four in new housing is that close to their place of employment.
- "Over two-thirds of older and historic neighbourhoods have an elementary school within one mile. Less than 40% of new construction does.
- "Over 60% of houses in older and historic neighbourhoods have shopping within one mile. Barely 40% of new houses do."

While this may be a fault of new design, it does demonstrate that the reuse of existing inner city accommodation for residential purposes also leads to an intensification of use of existing facilities, rather than increased pressure for new ones. Similar research (Holloway and Bunker, 2006) has been carried out in Australia, where two sites in Adelaide were investigated. The researchers looked at the delivered energy of two households, one on the city fringe and the other in an inner city.

Delivered energy is defined as operational energy and embodied energy used in dwellings and motor vehicles over their life cycles. There was a significant difference between the two locations, accounted for by the city fringe household consuming nearly twice as much energy in motorised travel. This tends to reinforce the argument in favour of city centre living, which is where older buildings tend to be located.

4.5 ENERGY PERFORMANCE OF HISTORIC BUILDINGS

It is not generally understood that historic buildings behave quite differently in environmental terms from modern buildings (Cassar, 2006). Walls and roofs may already be adequately insulated. Cassar considers that Chiswick House, built by Lord Burlington in the early 1720s, for example, may already have suitable environmental design features, without the need for complex technological solutions. She also makes the point that the historic environment is a finite and non-renewable resource, and for that reason alone it is sustainable to conserve it.

This is supported by the American experience. Park (1998: 1) writes:

"Historic architecture, particularly vernacular architecture, is by its very nature "green" because it is deeply tied to the land. The use of locally made materials; careful siting of buildings to take advantage of the prevailing winds and sun patterns; the reliance on natural systems of solar heating and ventilation utilizing physics of thermal mass and transport of air movement; and the use of durable materials means that many historic buildings already meet many of the principles outlined for new structures intended to be of a sustainable design."

It must be recognised, however, that such advantages of 'vernacular architecture', as described by Park (above) cannot all be applied to terraced housing, nor does the description deal with the economic drivers affecting the pathfinder areas.

In a report to the Energy Saving Trust (EST), Cambridge Architectural Research (CAR) (Palmer *et al.*, 2003: 2) claim that their research has *"destroyed once and for all the myth that it is better to rebuild than refurbish older housing to improve energy efficiency"*. It goes on to say (Palmer *et al.*, 2003: 2):

"The EST's current policy stance is that the UK should increase the annual replacement of dwellings from 15,000 to 50,000. In CAR's view this target is only viable if the 50,000 homes to be replaced have very poor energy performance and there are reasons apart from just energy efficiency that motivate replacement."

Case studies of five buildings in Dublin (Carrig Conservation, 2004) compared the actual cost of conservation and refurbishment with a desktop assessment of redevelopment. In most cases the straightforward repair/development cost was in favour of conservation. Life cycle costings and environmental impact assessments also came down in favour of conservation (see Section 6). As would be expected, the conservation option was more economic.

The counter-argument is made by the *40% house* (Boardman et al., 2005), which argues for the demolition of those older buildings with poor energy qualities, with the exception of a small number of buildings of acknowledged architectural merit.

Approximately 14% of the current housing stock would need to be demolished to meet this need, quadrupling the current rate of demolition. This study is based solely on the technical merits of the case, and does not take other factors into account. Discussing the *40% house*, David Ireland, Director of the Empty Homes Agency (Ireland, 2005: 1), writes that embodied energy in house building is a major source of energy.

"Normally it's about 90,000 kWh for a new family house. However a typical £40,000 refurbishment of a three-bedroom semi would normally only use 15,000 kWh of embodied energy."

A government report (DCLG, 2006) examines the housing stock and confirms that older buildings are lower rated in energy terms than buildings of more modern construction. It takes as its model for a 'large, hard to treat' dwelling a 1910s mid-terraced house, where the significant costs are double glazing and solid wall insulation.

Professor Anne Power of the London School of Economics advised the Treasury (Power, 2006: 1) that many such houses are in good structural condition, and are highly adaptable:

"The amounts of money needed for full repair, reinvestment and modernisation are invariably far lower than new build costs, offering greater durability (in spite of age) and lower maintenance costs than new build … Existing homes therefore need constant, relatively low level investment and occasional larger injections of capital."

This is borne out by a BRE report (Yates, 2006) that presents a method for assessing the refurbishment of traditionally built houses dating from 1840 to 1919, similar to that used in BREEAM EcoHomes. The methodology establishes a benchmark against which the benefits of various actions can be assessed, and in particular the competing requirements for modern energy and acoustic standards and whole building performance, including the effects of durability, reliability and maintainability of the building fabric. Refurbishment actions or interventions needed to raise the EcoHomes rating through six stages, from Poor to Exemplar, are defined against the economic, environmental and social limits for conservation and sustainability, beyond which actions become unacceptable in terms of damage to the built heritage or economically.

Based on case studies, the report shows that a range of refurbishment schemes can be successful in environmental and economic terms, but that there are limits to what can be achieved in a market-driven economy. The methodology is best used to compare a range of schemes, in order to select one that is most appropriate for the location and the needs of the local community, as part of an overall regeneration programme. Although the principles can be applied to houses in individual private ownership, the benefits are likely to take longer to materialise than when the project is implemented on a comprehensive basis by a housing association or local authority.

4.6   EMBODIED ENERGY

Buildings contain embodied energy, which inevitably is lost when a building is demolished. However, the balance between the embodied energy contained in a building and its operational energy consumption – the energy used for heating, air conditioning, lighting and power – is a complex relationship. Operational energy over the life of a building will be significantly greater than its embodied energy, as well as exceeding the costs of demolition and reconstruction. This point is made by Resurgence (2005: 1):

"[Embodied energy] can pale into insignificance when compared with the ongoing energy use over the lifetime of the buildings: the operational energy.

"Conserving energy use in buildings can be achieved through the use of more efficient insulation and power generation. But, of course, more insulation can itself increase the embodied energy, because some forms of insulation expend large amounts of energy during the manufacturing process – though the development of more natural insulation materials such as sheep's wool and recycled paper should, in time, ameliorate this. Victoria University in New Zealand (Alcorn and Wood, 1998) has calculated the embodied energy in various insulation products so that comparisons can be made, and these figures show that while fibreglass uses 269 kWh/m³, and polystyrene 650 kWh/m³ to produce, sheep's wool takes only 39 kWh/m³."

BS 7913 (British Standards Institution, 1998) reflects this and also makes the point that the improvement of the thermal properties of existing buildings means that the gap in performance between them and modern buildings can be narrowed.

"In environmental terms, the continued use of existing building stock, whether or not of particular architectural merit or historic interest, coupled with measures to improve energy efficiency, is a global priority. New build, by comparison, is a major user of non-renewable resources and energy." (BS 7913: 1998: 6.4.2)

BS 7913 also attributes the relative cheapness of new build to issues of scale, to mechanisation of the process, and to the relatively low cost of labour and resources involved in construction. The conservation and continued use of existing buildings, on the other hand, rely disproportionately on the relatively expensive and often scarce availability of skilled craftsmen and traditional building methods. Recognising the opportunities for maintaining existing buildings, and the fact that existing buildings are *"almost entirely benign in terms of toxicity"*, BS 7913 opines:

"However, improvements to the thermal insulation properties of existing buildings, to enable them to match the low levels of energy usage achieved in many new buildings, can often be difficult to achieve. In the case of

architecturally or historically important buildings, such improvements can often be impossible without alterations that can be unacceptably damaging in other ways. Nevertheless, in global environmental terms, the balance of advantage strongly favours the retention of existing building stock, particularly where performance in terms of energy consumption in use can be improved."

(BS 7913: 1998: 6.4.2)

There is a growing appreciation of the merits of traditional construction and, in particular, the thermal mass of solid stonewalls of significant thickness. According to English Heritage (2006: 5):

"Many traditional historic buildings perform well in energy terms. The thick walls and small windows of many pre-1900 vernacular buildings provide them with a high thermal mass, or capacitance, compared to 20th-century construction, which means that they can stay warmer in winter and cooler in summer ..."

Thermal mass is likely to be of advantage when it is taken into consideration with other issues to reduce energy consumption, such as improving the performance of boilers and appropriate regulation of heating controls, improving insulation and reducing draughts. According to Rypkema (2005: 4):

"Razing historic buildings results in a triple hit on scarce resources. First we are throwing away thousands of dollars of embodied energy. Second we are replacing it with materials which are vastly more consumptive of energy ... Third, recurring embodied energy savings increase dramatically as a building life stretches over 50 years. You're a fool or a fraud if you claim to be an environmentalist and yet you throw away historic buildings and their components."

4.7   THE VALUE OF CONSERVATION

Drivers Jonas (2006: 8), in advice to developers, says that:

"In residential use, well-converted or restored historic buildings are often much more valuable per square foot than new buildings. Blackheath is a good example of an area where the older houses are worth a lot more than the newer ones, partly on aesthetics, partly on quality of build. It is hard to think of many examples of good residential conversions being less valuable per square foot than new build residential."

For comparison, it is also worth noting that the investment performance of listed office buildings is at least equal to their non-listed (and, by implication, more modern) counterparts (see IPD 2002/2006).

The ODPM select committee (ODPM, 2004: 7) also noted evidence that commercial schemes that reuse historic buildings have a higher value than new-build developments, and can form the basis for regenerating a local economy. Chris Oldershaw (former Director of the Grainger Town Project) said in oral evidence to the committee:

"I think in many ways heritage and historic buildings have a crucial role to play in regeneration. They help to define the identity of cities; they also, certainly for Grainger Town, give economic and competitive advantages as well."

However, conserving old buildings can also mean conserving inappropriate and unattractive layout for both buildings and infrastructure and a balance needs to be struck between the advantages of conservation and of modern layout and infrastructure which may only be achievable with demolition.

4.8   SUMMARY

The literature has revealed a range of issues in support of refurbishment as a choice for dealing with low-demand or abandoned housing, much of which relies on the fact that such buildings are old and, by implication, well built, and make a valuable contribution both to the quality of housing within the locality and also to the sense of historic and social environment. The reduction of waste associated with refurbishment when compared with demolition and new construction, and the conservation of embodied energy and the reduction of pressure on the construction of modern building materials, contribute to the argument that refurbishment is more energy efficient.

However, if such powerful and widespread arguments support the policy of refurbishment, it is tempting to ask where the pressure to demolish and rebuild comes from.

It is implicit from some of the sources (eg CPRE, 2004; English Heritage, 2004) that at least some of the low demand or abandoned housing in the pathfinder areas is not worth saving, so demolition is the only option. What is important, however, is that such an assessment is made on objective and relevant criteria, so that principles of sustainability (however they are defined) are observed as far as possible.

What is also clear is that conservation/ refurbishment is not being market driven, despite the evidence that older dwellings are good value – cheaper than more modern properties and with a range of aesthetic and environmental qualities. It seems that it is only a limited section of the market that values such qualities; otherwise such properties would be priced at the higher end of the market range. It must also be suspected that the lack of suitable skills necessary to refurbish such properties sympathetically increases the costs and the inconvenience associated with appropriate repairs and maintenance, which in itself increases the burden and inconvenience of owning and maintaining such dwellings.

The trend to market a 'lifestyle' rather than a product probably also influences potential purchasers and tenants towards new dwellings and therefore away from much of the older housing stock, particularly traditional Victorian back-to-back housing. It is also likely that the opportunity to demolish and rebuild on a cleared site is more attractive, particularly to volume builders, than having to manoeuvre around existing structures. Such refurbishment is therefore likely to be more highly priced and time consuming for contractors, who might therefore wish to encourage decision-makers to opt for demolition and rebuild, rather than what so many commentators have recognised as a more sustainable option. However, this debate is continued in the next section.

5 DEMOLITION, NEW BUILD AND REFURBISHMENT COMPARED: WHICH IS THE MORE SUSTAINABLE OPTION?

5.1 INTRODUCTION

This section compares the two different models for the regeneration of areas of low demand and abandoned housing, which have been examined above:

1. demolition and new build (Section 3); and
2. refurbishment (Section 4).

There are several different criteria on which the two options can be compared (some of which have been discussed earlier). However, this section considers the two options in the light of specific economic factors:

- maintenance costs;
- performance of the housing stock;
- VAT; and
- sustainable construction.

5.2 MAINTENANCE COSTS

The point has already been made about the need to maintain historic dwellings in an appropriate and sympathetic manner (Sections 2.4.2 and 4.2). Also, a shortage of the skills necessary to deal with the fabric of such properties has been identified. Nevertheless, there is evidence that older dwellings are cheaper to maintain and occupy than newer dwellings.

For example, the ODPM (2004) highlights the English Heritage study surrounding three properties in the Manchester area of a similar size but different ages: a Victorian terraced house, a 1920s house, and one built in the 1980s. Maintenance and occupation costs were projected over a period of 100 years, looking at decoration, fabric maintenance, services maintenance, utility costs and insurance. Demand for heating and hot water, boiler efficiency and water services were assumed to be the same for all three houses. Largely as a result of the quality and lifespan of the materials used, maintenance and occupancy costs for the Victorian house were estimated at £2,648 per 100 m^2 per annum; for the 1920s house £3,112; and for the 1980s house £3,686. This work resulted in guidance from English Heritage (2005) on low-demand housing and the historic environment in the nine pathfinder partnerships.

Further research from English Heritage (2003) also indicates that older houses can cost less to maintain and occupy over the long term than modern dwellings.

According to Bevan and Dobie (2006: 18) who cite the earlier research "*on the basis of repair cost projections stretching over 30 years, the cost of repairing a Victorian terraced house is 40–60% cheaper … than replacing it with a new home.*"

5.3 PERFORMANCE OF THE HOUSING STOCK

A key rationale for the demolition of large areas of existing housing in some parts of the UK is claimed to be its poor environmental performance, along with the absence of demand for its continued ownership or occupation, and its non-compliance with modern Building Regulations. It has been documented by Bevan and Dobie (2006) that only 6% of the UK existing housing stock complies with today's building standards; yet, of the remaining 94%, very little falls into the category of low demand or abandoned properties, and thus would seem to remain attractive in the marketplace.

A report published by the ODPM (2003a) stated that approximately 6.5 million homes are classified as non-decent,[2] and 73% of these failed owing to inferior thermal comfort through inadequate insulation and heating systems. While the report suggests that the overall pattern of non-decent homes in the private sector has reduced, the proportion failing on thermal comfort has remained fairly constant at 60%. Furthermore, it is the owner-occupier market that is seemingly underperforming in terms of maintaining a decent standard. Figure 5.1, taken from the English Housing Condition Survey (ODPM 2003a), reports that over 45% of private rented and 25% of privately owned properties are non-decent. Given the high proportion of stock failing the 'decent' standards, housing improvement is clearly an urgent priority, and there needs to be a greater consideration by central government of the full range of viable solutions (Waters, 2006).

These figures suggest that there may be scope to radically improve the performance of UK housing through large-scale refurbishment. However, although much housing will be capable of benefiting from refurbishment, some old housing will be more challenging.

---

2 According to the Department for Communities and Local Government, a decent home should be warm, weatherproof and have reasonably modern facilities (CLG, 2007).

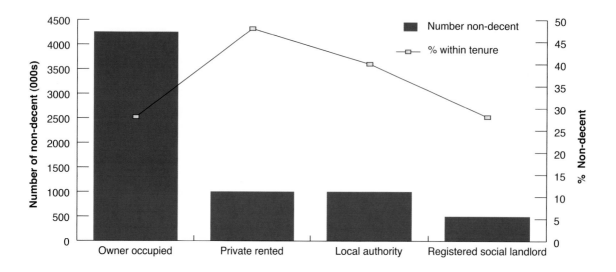

Figure 5.1: Number and percentage of non-decent homes, by tenure (2003)

Obstacles to refurbishment could include failing structures and materials, and obsolete and inconvenient layout, both of the interior of the building and of the building in relation to its immediate surroundings. Also relevant must be the local demand – or lack of demand – for accommodation, which could mean that money will be wasted if dwellings are refurbished but the interaction of market force results in there being no prospect of their attracting either a tenant or an owner-occupier. It is in relation to this section of the residential stock that the debate surrounding the choice between demolition and new build versus refurbishment becomes more critical.

5.4   VALUE ADDED TAX

It has long been recognised that the VAT regime treats new build and refurbishment differently, and dramatically affects their relative costs, because new build is currently zero rated. The VAT regime for home extensions and refurbishment is complicated. Normally VAT must be paid at the standard rate of 17.5%, but if a house has been empty for 10 years and is then refurbished, VAT may be recoverable. If a house has been empty for three years and is then refurbished, the VAT cost from 12 May 2001 is charged at the reduced rate of 5%. Further, where a building reconstruction involves retaining a single or double façade as a condition of planning consent, then the old building will be regarded as a new building and therefore is zero rated. Reduced-rate relief can also apply to conversions, but it is applied restrictively, and projects must meet strict definitions to be eligible (Baker Tilly, 2007).

Commentators (eg Anon, 1998; Bevan and Dobie, 2006: 20; Empty Homes Agency, undated), recognise that the VAT imbalance is a huge financial disincentive to the refurbishment of existing properties. The Empty Homes Agency (undated) argues that *"VAT provides a perverse*

incentive to neglect maintenance of existing homes…" Thus, even if all other considerations were equal in the choice between refurbishment and rebuild, the VAT implications would shift the financial advantage towards new build.

The Empty Homes Agency (undated) demonstrates the extent of the inequity thus:

"For example, Hyde Housing Association recently paid £120,000 in VAT on a project involving 21 homes. With a reduced rate of 5% VAT, they would have saved enough to refurbish another three homes."

Even as long ago as 1998, the RICS (Anon,1998) included in its 'Budget Wishlist' a plea for *"the Chancellor to cut the level of VAT on the refurbishment of existing property, thus reducing the advantage that new build has in the market"*.

The use of fiscal measures to benefit heritage conservation in Western Europe and North America was examined in research by Northumbria University (Pickard and Pickerill, 2007), including income tax credits for the provision of social housing in heritage buildings and VAT tax concessions. The research found that heritage tax incentives encourage individuals and corporations to act in socially desirable ways, although they do not compel such behaviour. Such tax incentives are most effective when used in conjunction with a national heritage regulatory policy, to ensure protection of important heritage assets. They are also highly efficient to operate, and encourage spending by property owners, occupiers and developers without requiring actual expenditure by government. The multiplier effects of spending on heritage conservation mean that the income forgone by government is recouped through increased tax revenue because of the positive impacts on neighbourhood revitalisation. The researchers conclude that, if used correctly, tax incentives can correct market failure and avoid costly and politically unpopular direct forms of government action.

Given the range of government policies that support sustainability criteria, it is illogical that Treasury policy should so disadvantage what is well recognised as the more sustainable option. Even if the Treasury were unwilling to lose revenue through removing the burden of VAT from refurbishment, it would still make sense for a similar level of tax to be applied to new build, so that the choice between the two was not one that might be decided purely on taxation grounds.

5.5 SUSTAINABLE CONSTRUCTION

It is widely recognised that buildings contribute to half of the UK's total CO_2 emissions, and that they also generate 16% of the nation's waste during the construction phase (Edwards and Turrent, 2000). Indeed, housing as a sector generated 27% of CO_2 emissions, second only to transport, according to BRECSU (see Figure 5.2).

Even if all future housing needs were capable of being met by the sustainable ideals launched by the government's SCP, the relative proportion of required new build is small when compared with the existing (and, in its current state, largely unsustainable) housing stock. The challenge is therefore to tackle the multifarious problems that need to be both identified and resolved in order to ensure that the older (pre-1990) housing stock is both eco-friendly and sustainable well into the 21st century.

The proposal within the SCP to meet the target of new dwellings in the new growth area of the South East of England has highlighted a significant flaw in the sustainability agenda, specifically that the construction of new dwellings has major sustainability disadvantages. This debate has relevance for the decisions being made in the pathfinder areas. For example, standard carbon emissions are 9.54 tonnes (tC) for the construction of a new dwelling, and, with a current build rate of 140,000 new homes per year, this could lead to 1.41 MtC being emitted into the atmosphere (Environmental Audit Committee, 2005).

Other potential impacts concern the environmental sustainability of using materials such as aggregates and timber, and the amount of waste generated, including contaminated soil and its disposal. In total, the housing sector generates some 30% of UK CO_2 emissions and emits 40 MtC into the atmosphere every year. Households currently consume 56% of all water supplied. In addition, the construction industry produces some 70 million tonnes of waste each year in the UK. Some 13 million tonnes of that comprise material which has been delivered to sites and thrown away unused (DETRb 2000: 10), with new build contributing significantly to carbon dioxide emissions. New house building can therefore create significant tensions within the sustainable development framework that is at the heart of the SCP, and which is also a major factor in the pathfinder area debate.

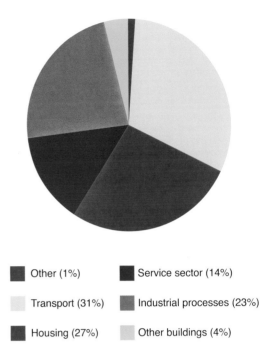

■ Other (1%)   ■ Service sector (14%)

□ Transport (31%)   ▨ Industrial processes (23%)

■ Housing (27%)   □ Other buildings (4%)

Figure 5.2: Carbon dioxide (CO_2) emissions by sector in the UK (BRECSU)

5.6 THE NATURE OF HOUSING REFURBISHMENT

The nature of the work required, and therefore the costs involved, in housing refurbishment projects varies widely, depending upon such factors as:

* the type of construction;
* the age, style, size and configuration of the existing accommodation;
* the original material specifications and the quality of the original construction; and
* the existing state of repair.

This being the case, it is therefore not possible to provide a generic detailed analysis of cost that will be generally applicable to all proposed new schemes. The work involved may range from, at one extreme, simply upgrading kitchens and bathrooms with minor alterations to plumbing and electrical services to, at the other, major rebuilds including foundation and other remedial structural stabilisation, rearrangement of the existing accommodation involving demolition and reconstruction of internal walls, floors and staircases, the construction of extensions, re-roofing, and the complete renewal of plumbing, heating and electrical systems. External works (roads, paving, fences etc), work required to external service mains (water, gas electricity, drainage and the like), and site abnormals (considered here to be any work necessary as a consequence of the site topography and geology, for example bulk excavation and filling, retaining walls, and special foundations) are always project specific, and their costs have therefore been excluded from the analysis presented here.

5.7 THE COSTS OF REFURBISHMENT COMPARED WITH NEW CONSTRUCTION

In reality, the costs for every prospective new project need to be examined in detail as an integral part of the initial feasibility study incorporating value management techniques to evaluate the overall value for money provided by the various feasible options. What is given here is simply an overall indication of the likely respective costs of refurbishment compared with new build.

A simple Building Cost Information Service (BCIS) database enquiry reveals that the overall average cost per m² of floor area for new housing is £694, compared with an average cost of £489 per m² for refurbishment. However, the range of values in the sample (£354–£1,351 per m² for 223 new-build projects and £269–£1,118 per m² for 21 refurbishment projects) means that these overall figures are not particularly useful, other than as a very general guide. Figure 5.3 shows a general breakdown of costs subdivided by different building types.

Figure 5.3 shows that across all four property types the average cost per m² for constructing a new building is greater than for refurbishing existing stock. The difference in cost is greatest for detached housing, where a new build is on average £606 per m² more expensive than a refurbishment. The smallest difference is for flats, where on average a new build is only £143 per m² more expensive. Figure 5.3 also shows that, in general terms:

- flats tend to be the most expensive building type per m², both to construct and to refurbish; and
- terraced and semi-detached houses tend to be, on average, more expensive per m² to refurbish than detached houses.

Figures based on data of this kind can, however, provide only an indication of likely costs. In order to present a clearer picture of the relative costs a more detailed examination of individual project analyses for refurbishment and for the construction of new housing was undertaken, the results of which are shown in Tables 5.1–5.4. All costs are normalised to first quarter 2007 prices with a UK mean location index applied, and the tender prices given are the costs of the buildings only, together with their proportion of preliminary costs. Projects chosen for analysis were mainly two-storey semi-detached and terraced houses, but a few of the projects selected also include some two-storey flats.

The refurbishment of medium- and high-rise properties (taken here as those of greater than two storeys) often comprises work of a very different nature from that involved in low-rise work, and is therefore not considered here.

The use of cost per m² values for refurbishment projects is frequently problematic, and potentially misleading, because of the possible inconsistencies in the way in which the overall areas are calculated. It is therefore considered more appropriate to examine the data on the basis of total cost per completed dwelling.

Refurbishment projects were subdivided into those comprising relatively minor work (eg refurbishment of kitchens and bathrooms, and minor alterations to building services; see Table 5.1) and those projects involving more complex work (see Table 5.2).

The data shown in Tables 5.1 and 5.2 indicate that the mean cost per dwelling for minor refurbishment work is £6,645 (minimum £5,456 (−18%), maximum £7,931 (+19.34%)). For major refurbishment the mean cost per dwelling is £45,314 (minimum £25,121, maximum £109,079). If, however, project no. 3 is discounted as unrepresentative of the sample as a whole, then the mean cost per dwelling is £36,204 (minimum £25,121 (−30.61%), maximum £48,343 (+33.53%)).

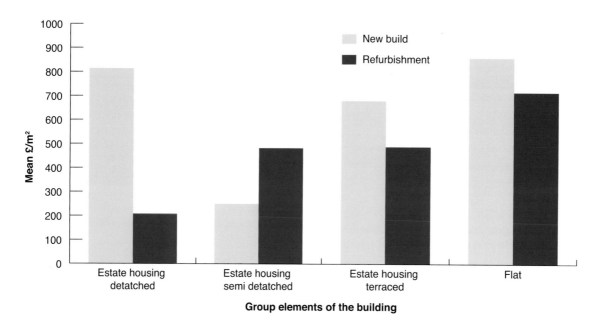

Figure 5.3: Comparison of the average £/m² for new build and refurbishment properties

For comparison, Table 5.3 shows the range of costs incurred in the conversion of a small number of other building types to form new dwellings, and Table 5.4 shows the costs of building new terraced housing over a range of projects.

Table 5.4 shows that, for the 19 projects selected for the study, the average cost per completed dwelling excluding external works and drainage was £75,297 (minimum £46,032, maximum £147,511), but if the outlying value (project 1) is again excluded, as it appears unrepresentative of the sample, then the average cost per dwelling falls to £71,285 (minimum £46,032 (−33.53%), maximum £94,196 (+32.14%)) (BCIS online, 2006).

Table 5.1: **Minimal refurbishment (refurbishment of kitchens and bathrooms, minor alterations to building services)**				
Project no	No of dwellings	Tender price (adjusted to 1stQ 2007 UK mean location)	Cost £/m²	Cost per refurbished dwelling
1	20	£113,050	£1,153	£5,653
2	103	£776,843	£732	£7,542
3	74	£586,899	£710	£7,931
4	263	£1,435010	£623	£5,456
Average cost/dwelling				£6,645
Minimum cost/dwelling				£5,456
Maximum cost/dwelling				£7,931

(Source: BCIS Online)

Table 5.2: **Major refurbishment (typically including structural repairs, re-roofing, new windows and doors, major alteration or replacement of heating and electrical installations)**				
Project no	No of dwellings	Tender price (adjusted to 1stQ 2007 UK mean location)	Cost £/m²	Cost per refurbished dwelling
1	17	£549,479	£428	£32,322
2	8	£264,314	£452	£33,039
3	22	£2,399,738	£1,037	£109,079
4	15	£427,068	£427	£25,121
5	68	£2,791,998	£597	£41,058
6	29	£1,069,381	£387	£36,875
7	74	£3,577,450	£484	£48,343
8	14	£513,407	£423	£36,671
Average cost/dwelling				£45,314
Minimum cost/dwelling				£25,121
Maximum cost/dwelling				£109,079

(Source: BCIS Online)

Table 5.3: **Costs of conversion of other types of building**				
Project no	No of dwellings	Tender price (adjusted to 1stQ 2007 UK mean location)	Cost £/m²	Cost per refurbished dwelling
1 (Dockside warehouse)	57	£10,654,448	£1,522	£186,920
2 (Church)	4	£944,516	£1,775	£236,129
3 (Farm buildings)	7	£878,138	£1,084	£125,448

(Source: BCIS Online)

Table 5.4:   Costs of new-build terraced housing

Project no	No of dwellings	Tender price (adjusted to 1stQ 2007 UK mean location)	Cost £/m²	Cost per refurbished dwelling
1	10	£1,475,112	£1,190	£147,511
2	8	£595,931	£934	£74,490
3	10	£764,412	£886	£76,441
4	9	£775,581	£1,049	£86,175
5	37	£2,929,266	£948	£79,169
6	38	£2,956,638	£909	£77,806
7	6	£565,179	£981	£94,196
8	36	£2,718,176	£759	£75,504
9	15	£690,490	£616	£46,032
10	24	£1,551,643	£825	£64,651
11	8	£531,064	£715	£66,383
12	5	£393,561	£974	£78,712
13	9	£518,766	£795	£57,640
14	13	£804,208	£752	£61,862
15	24	£1,555,632	£852	£64,818
16	47	£2,610,596	£618	£55,544
17	8	£507,927	£807	£63,490
18	10	£747,025	£797	£74,702
19	25	£2,136,247	£708	£85,449
Average cost/dwelling				£75,297
Minimum cost/dwelling				£46,032
Maximum cost/dwelling				£147,511

(Source: BCIS Online)

5.8   GROUP ELEMENT PRICES

Some analysis was also carried out to determine the relative distribution of the costs of refurbishment as against new construction for both flats and terraced housing. The data are based on the cost per m² of gross internal floor area and again excludes external works, drainage and contingencies, but includes a proportion of preliminaries costs.

Figures 5.4 and 5.5 show a comparison of refurbishment and new build of flats as a percentage of the total price of the scheme. Care should, however, be taken in interpreting these results, because a significant number of projects included in the sample are high-rise, system-built schemes, where the structural costs involved are likely to form a much higher proportion of total costs than would be the case with low-rise traditionally constructed projects.

Figures 5.6 and 5.7 show the costs of the different elements of the construction for new build and refurbishment of terraced housing, and Figures 5.8 and 5.9 show the costs relating to construction or refurbishment of a semi-detached house, but again the data provide only a general guide owing to the wide variation in the quantity of work required in the various refurbishment schemes.

The data for Figures 5.4–5.9 are based, according to BCIS sources, on the costs per m² of gross internal floor area for the buildings, excluding works and contingencies and with preliminaries apportioned by cost. Prices are as at the second quarter of 2006 (based on a tender price index of 233) and a UK mean location. Data were updated on 20 September 2006.

Key for figures 5.4 and 5.6

Substructure   Superstructure   Internal finishes   Fitting   Services

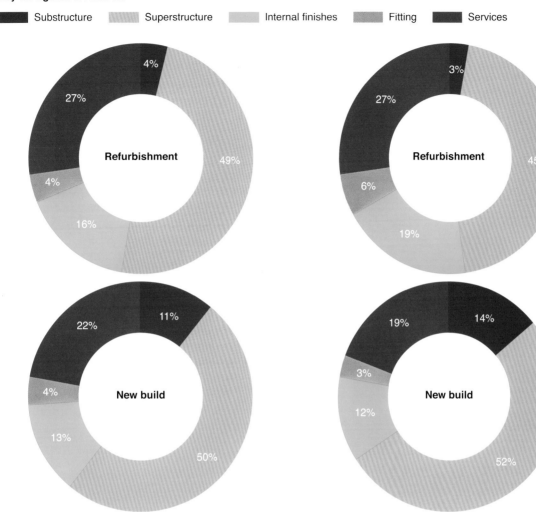

Figure 5.4: Comparison of the group element prices for refurbishment and new build flats as a percentage of the total price of the scheme

Figure 5.6: Comparison of the group element prices for refurbishment and new build terraced houses as a percentage of the total price of the scheme

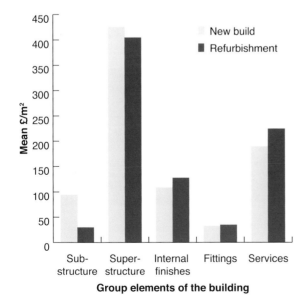

Figure 5.5: Comparison of the average group elements £/m² for new build and refurbishment flats

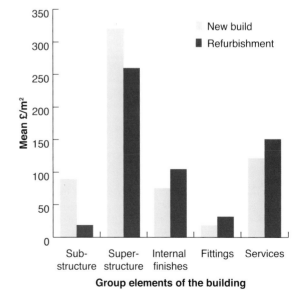

Figure 5.7: Comparison of the average group elements £/m² for new build and refurbishment terraced houses

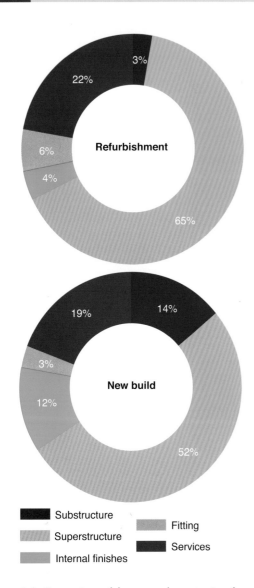

Figure 5.8: Comparison of the group element prices for refurbishment and new build semi-detached houses as a percentage of the total price of the scheme

5.9 COMPARISON OF UNIT COSTS

Figure 5.3 shows that across all four property types the average costs per m² for constructing a new building are greater than for refurbishing the existing stock. The difference in cost is greatest for detached housing, where a new build is, on average, £606/m² more expensive than a refurbishment. The smallest difference is for flats, where on average a new build is only £143/m² more expensive. It should be noted that 'flats' include the conversion of large dwellings into a number of smaller units, thereby reducing expenditure on structures and the foundations, as they are pre-existing.

In Figure 5.10 the properties are ranked in order of cost to build or refurbish, and it can be seen that flats are the most expensive property type for both building methods. However, the remaining building types are ranked in completely different orders.

For new builds, a detached house is more expensive to construct than a terraced house, showing that the building costs can be shared for a development involving numerous joined properties better than for a development of detached housing. The saving would be seen in having to build fewer walls, having one continuous roof, and having shared main services supplies, such as sewage pipes.

The reverse, however, is true for the refurbish option, where a terraced house is on average more expensive to redevelop than a detached property. This is possibly as a result of those schemes where the design and layout of the terraced housing have been reconfigured, sometimes involving two houses being knocked into one to create a larger home, which might be more attractive to the market, whereas the refurbishment of a detached house may involve fewer structural alterations.

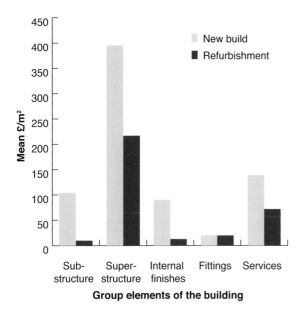

Figure 5.9: Comparison of the average group elements £/m² for new build and refurbishment semi-detached houses

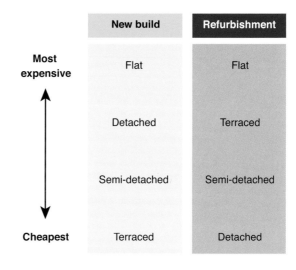

Figure 5.10: Relative construction costs for new and refurbished property

5.10 SUMMARY

Analysis of the BCIS data shows that on average it is more expensive to build new properties than to refurbish existing buildings, and that this is true across all types of residential property (detached, semi-detached, terraced and flats). However, the difference in the costs varies with the property type being considered, except that flats are the most expensive type of residential building for both new builds and refurbishments.

On the basis of the evidence gathered from the database, in the case of terraced and semi-detached estate housing the cost of a minimal level of refurbishment (equivalent to upgrading of kitchens and bathrooms to meet the decent homes standard), at first quarter 2007 prices, is likely to vary between approximately £5,500 and £8,000, with a project average of approximately £6,600.

More complex refurbishment, such as that potentially required to upgrade Victorian terraced housing, including some structural repair, re-roofing, some internal rearrangement, new windows and doors, the replacement of kitchen and bathroom fittings, rewiring and the installation of new central heating, is likely to cost between £25,000 and £50,000, depending upon the scale of the work required. The average cost for the schemes examined in this study was approximately £36,200 per dwelling.

Conversion of other building types to form new dwellings can be expected, on the basis of the projects considered in this study, to cost of the order of £125,000–£200,000 per dwelling.

For new build, semi-detached and terraced estate housing may reasonably be expected to cost between approximately £45,000 and £95,000 per dwelling (between £620 and £1,000 per m² of internal floor area) with an average cost of approximately £71,000 per dwelling.

Note, however, that, as explained earlier, the top end of the refurbishment spectrum at £50,000 per dwelling overlaps the bottom end of the new-build spectrum at £45,000 per dwelling, and particular care therefore needs to be taken to carry out detailed cost and value management studies as integral elements of the project feasibility study.

This analysis of the BCIS data reflects only the costs spent at the point of construction or refurbishment; it does not take into account the costs in use of the dwellings during the periods of occupation. In terms both of economic and of environmental costs, it is important to factor in such life cycle costs as are incurred during the life of the buildingto any comparison between refurbishment and new build, and this is the subject of the next section.

6 SUSTAINABILITY INDICATORS AND ASSESSMENTS

6.1 INTRODUCTION

The previous section compared the initial costs of new build and refurbishment for a range of dwelling types. However, the true cost of each process must also reflect the subsequent costs of occupation. Some form of life cycle cost analysis (LCCA) is therefore fundamental in the new build/refurbishment comparison.

There is a great deal of confusion surrounding the terminology used in life cycle cost analysis. For the purpose of this report, life cycle cost analysis and whole life costing analysis (WLCA) are synonymous, although both are used in the literature according to the authors' preference.

Fuller (2005: 1) defines LCCA thus:

"Life-cycle cost analysis (LCCA) is a method for assessing the total cost of facility ownership. It takes into account all costs of acquiring, owning and disposing of a building or building system. LCCA is especially useful when project alternatives that fulfil the same performance requirements, but differ with respect to initial costs and operating costs, have to be compared. … LCCA is not useful for budget allocation."

Fuller also defines lowest life cycle cost (LCC) as *"the most straightforward and easy-to-interpret measure of economic evaluation"*.

Life cycle cost analysis is a method used to estimate the overall costs of project alternatives with the aim of selecting *"the design that ensures the facility will provide the lowest overall cost of ownership consistent with its quality and function. The LCCA should be performed early in the design process while there is still a chance to refine the design to ensure a reduction in life-cycle costs (LCC)"* (*ibid.*).

The UK government has decided that all construction procurement choices will be made on the basis of whole life costs, in order to achieve long-term economic systems and buildings, describing the *"lowest cost now"* culture as being incompatible with long-term profitability (Langmaid, 2006). Thus:

"The capital cost of a building or the services within a building is only a part – and a small part – of the total economic pie. The operating and maintenance costs associated with that capital cost can outweigh the initial investment several times over." (Langmaid 2006: 1)

Langmaid (2006) recognises that there is great deal of uncertainty surrounding what whole life costing is, what it does, and what it can be used for. He states:

"… whole life costing analysis is a method of project economic evaluation in which all costs arising and benefits accrued from installing, owning, operating, maintaining, and ultimately disposing of a project are considered to be potentially important to that decision." (*ibid.*: 1)

He also states that its objective is to provide the decision-maker with sufficient information on which to base a reasoned judgement, and recognises the importance of involving the client early on in the decision-making process.

The use of WLCA is being restricted within the construction industry because:

"Major client institutions separate and fund capital costs and running costs into separate budgets; and manufacturers of capital equipment are unable to provide cost and longevity data in sufficient detail and with sufficient contextual information to enable the recurring operational and maintenance costs and periodicity to be accurately measured." (Langmaid, 2006: 2)

According to Langmaid (2006: 2) WLCA has not been generally implemented within the UK because:
* of the ignorance of the client;
* capital and running costs are not clearly separated along the lines of capital and operational expenditure familiar to most companies;
* there is no framework for collecting relevant data, together with the techniques for adjusting rule-of-thumb data to individual projects; and
* buildings are generally non-standard and complex, and there is no traditional close-knit partnership between all parties, which is necessary to evaluate the relationship between the various different services and structural elements involved.

However, it is recognised (*ibid.*) that clients are seeking buildings that have the lowest possible whole life cost, together with the longest service life attainable within other parameters, the highest possible quality, the best appearance, and the least taxation. It is therefore important that clients are involved within the strategic decision-making stage, and especially in decisions that involve trade-offs between functional requirements, technical viability, economic performance and environmental impact.

Case studies of five buildings in Dublin (Carrig Conservation, 2004) compared the actual cost of conservation and refurbishment with a desktop assessment of redevelopment. In most cases the straightforward repair/development cost was in favour of conservation. Life cycle costings and environmental impact assessments also came down in favour of conservation (see Section 4.5). As would be expected, given the lower conservation requirement, the conservation option was more economic.

These case studies also reinforce the point that the operational energy costs of a building outrun the embodied energy costs of the building's lifetime:

"In most cases, the costs involved in servicing and running built facilities during their lifetime far exceed the initial costs of construction."

Thus, to evaluate the refurbish/new build option on initial costs alone is to consider only a small proportion of the costs and benefits that will result from the decision, and it is important that decision-makers are aware of this.

6.2   FACTORS INFLUENCING DEVELOPERS' DECISION-MAKING

Recent research has implied that for sustainable construction and development to truly work, there has to be an economic appreciation and strong business case put forward (Carter, 2006; Ellison and Sayce, 2007), and as the term 'sustainability' encroaches increasingly upon our daily lives, it has been transformed into phrases of varying form and multiple meanings. In this report we take the simple definition of sustainable construction, as reported in Carter (2006: 2), to be:

"...meeting the challenge of supplying homes which are not only economically viable and desirable, but also encourage a sense of community and use natural resources efficiently".

The key challenge, nevertheless, is how developers are to address the increasing sustainability legislation cost-effectively. For instance, the increased use of combined heat and power (CHP) and grey water recycling represents a major shift in the incorporation of sustainable design in residential development.

Carter (2006) discusses the broad factors that will be considered when assessing the viability of a development project. Figure 6.1 shows a diagrammatic representation of this.

The costing process shown in Figure 6.1 is a simplified representation of the factors that should be considered throughout a residential development project, and it is at these main stages of the development process where most control is present. Opportunities for significant financial savings from a focus on sustainability are most likely to occur during the design and construction process. For instance, landfill tax is a considerable expense (see Section 3.3).

Environmentally sound building materials have also become more popular amongst professionals owing to the global increase in construction activity and the rising costs of transport (through increases in oil prices, for instance). The cost of timber, for example, has reduced significantly over the last eight to ten years (Carter, 2006). It is unclear whether the popularity of such materials results from their green or economic credentials, or both.

Increased construction costs have also seen developers turning to new ways of adapting the traditional production line. Modern methods of construction and off-site production techniques are being used to improve the competitive advantage of residential property development, and these new processes should alleviate some of the pressures and escalating costs associated with brownfield redevelopment.

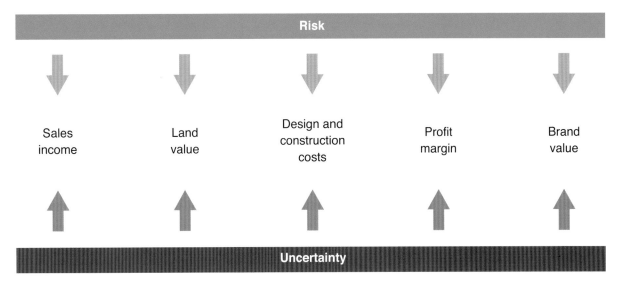

Figure 6.1: Main decision-making criteria in residential property development

Several developers have expressed the opinion that MMC, set up in accordance with a 'Fordist'-type manufacturing process, will *"drive down the costs of construction"* (discussed in Dixon *et al.*, 2005). The benefits of applying MMC are summarised in a case example based on an operational factory of a large volume house builder (Case study 2). Urban Splash and Westbury Homes (through their Space 4 initiative) are trialling off-site construction techniques in order to minimise their exposure to material price fluctuations, skills shortages, delays caused by weather, as well as to ease compliance with the recently modified Parts L and E of the Building Regulations (Dixon *et al.*, 2005).

However, according to Dixon *et al.* (2005) the economic restrictions involved in the application of MMCs are well known. A developer survey (Dixon *et al.*, 2005) undertaken at the College of Estate Management found that there was a general appreciation of the fact that MMCs are cost-effective only in volume. One developer suggested that:

"Modern methods of construction will come down to volume and how much that production line can cope with … the greater the volume the greater reduction in cost." (Dixon et al., 2005: 91)

Within the same report, a medium-volume house builder felt that the regulation of supply and demand would be complicated if a developer became reliant upon MMCs, and expressed concern that the overall control of supply and demand was reduced by off-site manufacturing. The same house builder stated:

"I don't want to build more than I can sell. If you have got the volume quota it is fine, but in the general market I don't think I could predict that. Housing market sales have taken a big dip this year – why would I want an order of 200 houses in a factory to come to me? What am I going to do with them?" (Dixon et al., 2005: 91)

Furthermore, the use of MMCs is a relatively new government- and industry-led initiative. The investment of capital and time in implementing these new techniques was therefore seen as a barrier, alongside the associated risk. One developer stated:

"There is a time lag, a learning curve that is going to cost us money, and it is a risk where you implement a new technique … things may go wrong." (Dixon et al., 2005: 92)

The greatest constraint is the lack of skills in the industry to implement innovation. The survey highlighted an overall awareness of the fact that the supply of a new, skilled workforce was not forthcoming. There was also agreement amongst developers that young people are no longer interested in employment in the construction sector. A lack of training programmes to encourage employment and new apprentices is apparent, as is the unattractive image of the industry to potential recruits.

Case study 2: Case example – modern methods of construction

- £20m cost to set up production line (off-site manufacturing factory)

- Production capacity of 5,000 dwellings per annum

- Web-enabled supply chain management facilitates just-in-time production

- Timber frame = quicker build but costs inflated

- Benefits of accelerating process > addition build cost

- Total build time reduced from 16–20 weeks to 6–8 weeks (bricklaying is taken off the critical path so internal fitting-out can progress in parallel)

(Source: Westbury Homes
– 'Space 4' www.westbury.plc.uk/Company/Space4/)

As a consequence, the drive towards using prefabrication and other new construction techniques is associated with an industry-wide initiative to 'de-skill the process'. As one developer stated:

"… it's just extremely difficult to get the labour. If you wanted an extra 20,000 homes I don't think we could provide it … well, other than by coming from a factory and being stacked up." (Dixon et al., 2005: 93)

Thus MMCs are being seen as a suitable alternative to traditional methods of production amidst ever-increasing labour and construction costs. In summary, the interview results (Dixon *et al.*, 2005: 93) showed that:
- innovation in the development sector is industry-wide, and not specific to brownfield regeneration;
- adaptations of existing building techniques, such as piling, which aims to reduce soil movement (and disturbance of potential contaminants), may have been stimulated by the focus on brownfield development;
- techniques used in the commercial sector are seemingly being taken up by the house-building industry. However, at present this process is limited; and
- at present, there are several constraints on innovation in the development industry, and the skills shortage is perhaps of greatest concern.

These results, taken from the College of Estate Management's report (Dixon *et al.*, 2005), provide a very concise overview of the UK development industry's feelings towards new innovation and sustainable construction techniques. They provide a good basis from which to develop ideas and opinion within this report.

Many practitioners and developers consider that the drive to and increased uptake of sustainable construction and design have come from the understanding that consumers are increasingly conscious about energy saving and conservation strategies. Waters (2006) explained that, amidst a climate of rising energy costs, the need for energy-efficient product availability, in both new and older property, is becoming increasingly important. This is likely to be advanced through the introduction of energy performance certificates, a mandatory component of a pre-sale house survey report, introduced in June 2007. It is therefore argued that addressing sustainability through a branding or rigorous marketing campaign can significantly enhance the reputation of a development scheme. Urban Splash, with the launch of their New Islington residential development in East Manchester, has demonstrated this type of eco-marketing. Equally, on the other side of the spectrum, non-compliance with environmental best practice may be detrimental to the reputation and therefore to the success of a scheme, as well as to the developer itself.

Market demand, as in other sectors, will largely dictate the uptake of new technologies and sustainable design for residential properties. The property profession is still viewing eco-property (particularly within the residential sector) largely as a niche market; although changes in the trading process through introductions such as energy rating assessments are likely to expand the market for 'good' environmental performance over the next five to ten years. With specialist companies establishing themselves, and with market products and renewable energy sources offering cost-effective solutions to rising energy bills and continually rising levels of CO_2 emissions, the movement towards sustainable construction (however that is defined) is likely to continue to gather pace.

Carter (2006: 8) notes three key factors influencing the decision-making process and the potential of a building for reuse:

- Structural integrity. The structure should be in good condition: eg the extent of work required to reuse a severely decayed building could cause it to not be cost-effective;
- Historical value. Structures of historic value should be considered very carefully for reuse in order to maintain architectural style, diversity and wider social and environmental benefits; and
- the building should initially be considered for a similar use.

Market structure was also seen as an important secondary consideration, suggesting that consideration has to be given to the local housing market and to whether consumers will demand sustainable features within the homes they occupy.

6.3 ASSESSMENT TOOLS AND CRITERIA

As with commercial property, the ownership of residential units is transferred to the end user, and unless sustainability features command a premium in the market, there is little incentive for developers to consider the range of sustainable measures, such as reduced energy consumption. This has restricted progress on the introduction and monitoring of sustainability during phases of construction.

Historically, the UK construction industry has focused on the initial and economic cost of project delivery. The UK government is increasingly attempting to control the environmental standard of residential property through the planning system, most recently by the introduction of sustainable building codes, working alongside existing EcoHomes ratings. The Code for Sustainable Homes, launched in 2005, seeks to rate the environmental performance of buildings on a one to six star scale (with the highest rating representing 'carbon neutral').

This debate suggests that more certainty is required in decision-making processes when assessing individual sites for development potential and, more importantly, the options for the retention of existing stock or the prospects for its replacement with new-build development. It seems clear that both options require an appreciation of innovative sustainable construction and day-to-day operational efficiency in order to meet the objectives of sustainable development. Hence the measurement of progress is fundamental, and this can be achieved only with the use of a suitable set of indicators. Furthermore, it has been acknowledged by the CIOB that sound monitoring tools for practitioners to assess sustainability may be a competitive advantage in the marketing of eco-property.

Decision-making for residential construction operates according to the policies and practices of particular developers, although often monetary issues are dominant (Ellingham and Fawcett, 2006). However, other considerations such as building design and sustainability are incorporated into today's decisions as a requirement of efficient investment – that is, under- or overinvestment – and with a socially responsible investment (SRI) strategy (Lützkendorf and Lorenz, 2005; Ellison and Sayce, 2007).

Table 6.1 gives an overview of the tools most commonly used by UK developers when assessing sustainable construction and sustainable development.

A suitable amount of progress is also being made with the establishment of a common set of indicators to measure the sustainability of residential development projects in the UK, although it seems that these are being criticised for lacking clear objectivity and for offering an inadequate amount of information for sound management (refer, for example, Lowe and Bell, 2000).

Table 6.1: Assessment methods for sustainable construction

Tool kit	Brief description
Bequest	This is an international framework designed to offer a tool or procurement protocol to support decision making for a sustainable built environment. It uses a variety of indicators and gives consideration to relevant environmental and sustainable development issues. It examines sustainability (eg ecological integrity, community participation, futurity of plans, cultural heritage and forms of settlement) in relation to key stages of the construction process, examining, for instance, key issues, consultations, procurement methodologies and monitoring itself.
Considerate Constructors Scheme (CCS)	This scheme was introduced in 1997 to improve the image of the construction industry and is a voluntary code of practice for those involved in a construction site to sign up to. The code commits those in the scheme to be considerate and good neighbours, as well as clean, respectful, safe, environmentally conscious, responsible and accountable. The scheme is administered by the site advertising with posters that they are part of the CCS and inviting members of the public to contact the site manager of scheme's office if they have a comment or complaint about the site, which will lead to a set of disciplinary procedures being followed.
EcoHomes	This is predominantly used for new builds or major refurbishments and assesses the environmental performance of residential dwellings. Assessment is undertaken both at the design stage, which gives the opportunity to make adjustments to the specifications before work starts, and post-construction, to monitor the achievements. The scheme establishes best practice criteria for a broad range of environmental issues ranging from climate change, use of resources, impacts on wildlife and the need for a high quality internal environment. Licensed assessors compare developments on a rating system of pass, good, very good or excellent. It is perhaps the most commonly used assessment tool by UK house builders.
EcoHomes XB	EcoHomes XB is designed as a tool to assist registered social landlords (RSLs) and housing associations in planning and prioritising their maintenance and refurbishment works by highlighting properties that are in need of attention.
	The Building Research Establishment (BRE) has recently published a new methodology for the assessment of environmental performance for existing buildings. The tool kit, launched in May 2006*, is designed for property professionals to assess the improvement works required on existing stock and may also be useful in identifying the potential for refurbishment. As highlighted by Bagenholm (2006), EcoHomes XB is organised around a number of environmental measures and sustainability indicators, which are set out below:
	Assessment of topics covered by EcoHomes XB (Bagenholm, 2006): • Management policies – Energy efficiency, environmental policy, and energy labelling; • Energy – Fabric loss, energy-efficient fittings, heating system controls, SAP ratings, drying space, external lighting; • Transport – Access to public transport; • Pollution – Zero emission energy source; • Water – Internal water use, external water use; • Health – External private space, internal private space, controlled ventilation; and • Waste – Reduction of material waste, domestic recycling facilities and disposal of appliances.
	EcoHomes XB assesses minor works and minor refurbishments using desktop assessment evaluating the overall environmental performance. Assessment also targets improvements that can be made. Essential data required include: • Property type, eg detached, terraced, semi-detached; • Property age, eg pre-1919, 1921, 1957; • Number of units being assessed; and • SAP rating (refer Section 6.3.5).
	It is organised around a number of environmental measures and indicators including: management policies (energy efficiency and labelling); energy (fabric loss, heating systems, SAP rating); access to public transport; pollution (zero emission energy sources); water usage; health (internal and external private spaces, controlled ventilation) and waste reduction/management.
	This tool is used to measure impacts of existing property, recognising small-scale improvements over time. It includes building fabric, fixtures and structures already in situ. EcoHomes XB also incorporates a management section that looks at companies' bespoke requirements. This latest addition to the EcoHomes portfolio will mean that there are two complementary methodologies to examine new build and existing stock.
Envest	Envest 2 is a web-based tool, designed to simplify calculations relating to the environmental and whole life costs of building, allowing for easier comparison to be made about different strategies in a way that allows for the environmental and financial trade-offs to be fully understood. A building's design elements are input (height, roof covers, number of storeys, etc.), and the system identifies which element has the greatest environmental impact and allows for the effects of choosing different materials to be seen. The system can also be used to evaluate different strategies of heating, cooling and operating the building.

Table 6.1: **Assessment methods for sustainable construction (contd.)**

Environmental Profiling	BRE's methodology for environmental profiling of construction materials was introduced in 2001 and allows for the independent assessment of construction materials and products in terms of their environmental performance in both their manufacture and use. The scheme works by way of certification, which can be used to demonstrate a company's environmental performance. The profile is based on 13 environmental indicators and a BRE Ecopoints score, which compares the environmental impact of the product against the impact of a typical person in the UK for a year.
SAP	This is the UK Government's Standard Assessment Procedure (SAP) for the energy rating of residential buildings and forms part of the national methodology for calculating the energy performance of buildings to show compliance with Part L of the Building Regulations (England and Wales). A SAP rating is required for both new homes and dwellings undergoing significant alterations (such as an extension).
	Originally introduced during the 1990s, SAP extended the notion of whole building performance-based regulation when, from 1995, all dwellings were required to have a SAP rating (Bell and Lowe, 2000: 31).
	SAP was also recognised as a compliance method in its own right.
	Within Part L of the Building Regulations (concerned with reducing energy consumption) the traditional approach has been to focus on the performance of the building envelope by the specification of maximum elemental U-values. This, however, ignored heating performance, an oversight which was rectified in 1990 when 'whole house' calculation procedures were introduced. Bell and Lowe (2000: 31) comment that:
	'This method allows considerable trade-off between elements of the thermal envelope, the space and water heating systems, the fuel used and the fuel tariff.'
	The effect of this has, however, been to introduce 'considerable ambiguity and variation in standard depending on the method chosen to demonstrate compliance' (*ibid.*). Bell and Lowe (2000: 34) criticise the complexity of the method and the high costs of demonstrating compliance and, conclude with the following:
	'... first, the different methods of compliance do not possess a high degree of equivalence; second, the considerable scope which exists for trade-off between the insulation of the thermal envelope and the efficiency of energy systems is difficult to justify given the need to reduce CO_2 emissions in the long term; and third, the SAP index does not relate directly to energy consumption or environmental impact.'
	It should be noted that Bell and Lowe's work relates to new build, but they recognise (2000: 35) that the capacity of the Building Regulations to tackle the existing housing stock is limited, but an important issue for the environmental policy.
	They suggest that further amendment to Part L in the definition of a material alteration could allow scope for improvement in the energy efficiency standards of repairmodernisation works.
	SAP 2005 is adopted by government as part of the UK's national methodology for calculating the energy performance of buildings. It is used to demonstrate the compliance of dwellings with Part L of the Building Regulations (England and Wales) and to provide energy ratings for dwellings. The method of calculating the energy performance and the ratings is set out in the form of a worksheet, accompanied by a series of tables. The methodology is compliant with the Energy Performance of Buildings Directive. The calculation should be carried out using a computer program which is linked to a worksheet and is approved for SAP calculations. A SAP rating is required for all new build dwellings and those which are undergoing significant material alteration (such as the addition of an extension to the dwelling).
Sustainable Building Codes	This is a voluntary initiative launched in 2005, aimed at promoting changes in construction practices which are designed to be more sustainable. It requires that buildings use energy, water and other materials more efficiently and that the practices are designed to safeguard occupants' health and well-being. The goal of the codes is that they will become the national standard for sustainable building, which is demanded by consumers. The Code for Sustainable Buildings, launched in 2005, seeks to rate the environmental performance of buildings on a 0 to 5* scale (with the highest rating representing 'carbon neutral'). However, at present these codes suffer from a nonmandatory status as well as the challenge of addressing the environmental performance of older stock. Nonetheless, the principal objective of the code is for them to become the single national standard for sustainable building that all sectors of the building industry will subscribe to and that consumers will demand.

* Further information on EcoHomes XB is on the BREEAM website www.breeam.org/page.jsp?id=25.

6.4 CRITIQUE OF SUSTAINABILITY INDICATORS

The concept of socio-economic indicators is not new, and their use to inform policy decisions dates back to the mid-1960s (Hemphill et al., 2004a). The availability of more sophisticated data has seen the use of indicators diversify into the land use planning and regeneration industry. As discussed by Hemphill et al. (2004a), the assessment of the effectiveness of regeneration policy and practice has been the subject of numerous evaluations.

Hemphill et al. (2004b) identify other examples of useful indicators relating to the built environment: the ratio of open space to built form; reclamation of contaminated land; commercial viability; quality of final product; quality of public space; and usage of public space as well as the quality of private space.[3] They go on to conclude that the evaluation of regeneration initiatives is acknowledged to be an essential part of delivering holistic, sustainability-led strategy. However, their paper concludes that the attitudes of property professionals must change before sustainable urban regeneration (SUR) and other indicator-based assessments can be fully supported. This is why there should be continual evaluation of case study examples.

According to the Audit Commission (2002), urban policy and regeneration programmes are increasingly following an indicator approach; and a baseline assessment is usually undertaken to assess the effects of policy actions. Nonetheless, it is problematic to extend this rationale to more specific sustainability criteria (quality of life, community enterprise and social stability). The paper goes on to highlight the complexities of incorporating the three pillars of sustainability (environmental, economic and social), which have led to some degree of uncertainty:

"...sustainability indicators can be meaningful provided they are applied at the appropriate level, although there is a lack of a consensus in the literature about what indicators should be used to measure sustainability and how these indicators should be measured and scored." (Hemphill et al., 2004b: 10)

The use of indicators offers the opportunity to improve the knowledge, practice and achievement of sustainability for the UK property profession, by providing tools for analysis, mediation or decision-making (Balsas, 2004: 4). In addition, increased environmental awareness has brought a need to employ indicators as a key mechanism for assessing the environmental impact (as discussed by Wong, cited in Hemphill et al., 2004a). They can be useful in terms of long-term planning and development appraisal. Key performance indicators (KPIs) are being used in an increasing number of development projects and government policies, although they have been criticised for lacking a clear organisation of objectives, and for being inadequate in terms of information for

coherent management (Likierman, 1993). In light of these criticisms, Kotval (2001) and subsequently Hollander (2002) identified the following criteria that KPIs for sustainability must meet:

1. Relevance and impact: the indicator must be relevant;

2. Validity and availability: indicators must be objective, statistically defensible, credible, and able to be reproduced affordably in the future;

3. Simplicity and clarity: the data and indicators must be understandable to the general public and policy-makers;

4. Ability to aggregate information: indicators must be capable of relating to broader issues of sustainability;

5. Ability to reflect trends: the output should help determine long-term impact and trends over time;

6. Consistency and reliability: data should be searchable reliably over time;

7. Measurability: data should be easily and freely obtainable;

8. Cost-effectiveness: data collection and analysis should not be prohibitively expensive; and

9. Comparability: general data sources should be cross-comparable.

In the measurement of sustainable development it is critical that any information presented is explicitly stated, and translated into convenient units of information. Currently, a national programme is being established in Switzerland, called MONET (SFSO, 2002), which is seeking to develop an indicator system for monitoring sustainable development. This is a set of codes that derives from three broad categories: 'social solidarity', 'economic efficiency' and 'environmental responsibility'. In terms of housing provision, MONET considers factors such as floor area per person, contentment with housing conditions, income spent on housing, restoration activity, and density.

Bell and Lowe (2000) argue that a significant improvement in the Building Regulations is required if large reductions of CO_2 emissions are to be achieved during the first half of the 21st century. They report that improvements of 50% or more are possible for many existing buildings, particularly those with masonry cavity wall construction, and that 90% reductions in space heating are achievable.

Bell and Lowe (2000: 30) point out some problems with the comparability of standards internationally; for example, the method of calculating U-values in Denmark and Sweden is much more stringent than in the UK.

---

3   This balances the development that has occurred and the quality of that development in accordance with sustainability principles.

6.5 SUMMARY

Given the drive for sustainability within the construction process (both new build and refurbishment), and the mandatory requirement for energy efficiency certificates for the sale of dwellings, it is increasingly important to develop, promote and use clear, accurate and flexible methodologies to assess energy efficiency within dwellings.

Such methodologies need to be both accurate – to the extent that they measure what they purport to measure – and effective in achieving the desired (and stated) outcome. It would also be helpful if they could be based on internationally agreed measurement standards so that comparisons can usefully be undertaken.

Similarly, if the government is serious about reducing CO_2 emissions in dwellings, then something more than mandatory codes needs to be introduced. Incorporating such standards within the Building Regulations and extending those to instances of minor works and refurbishment are important demonstrations of that commitment, both to the industry and to the wider public. The provision for grant aid would also demonstrate the government's concern for both the maintenance and the improvement of the nation's housing stock as well as for the wider environment.

The literature has made it clear that housing is second only to transport in its generation of CO_2 emissions, and the the general public's increasing awareness of both the sustainability agenda and the ever-rising costs of fuel is increasing the concern for energy efficiency in the home. Of course, energy efficiency is not merely about the existence of suitable materials, insulation, and equipment. It is also about optimising their uses, so that maximum benefits are achieved: this involves further public education, in terms both of the appropriate use of individual dwellings and of more general campaigns for energy saving.

7 SURVEY RESULTS AND ANALYSIS

7.1 BACKGROUND AND RESEARCH QUESTIONS

This section of the report presents findings from a national postal survey of house builders (both private and social), and professional advisers working on housing development projects, including architects, building surveyors and quantity surveyors. The survey, undertaken in November–December 2006, gathered opinion about the drive towards sustainable housing development. The research questionnaire focused on the following key themes:

1. the redevelopment versus refurbishment debate;
2. attitudes towards sustainable development;
3. the use of sustainable construction techniques; and
4. measuring sustainable development and construction.

Specifically, the following questions were addressed:
- To what extent have developers and their professional advisers embraced new tools, such as EcoHomes and the UK Building Codes, for measuring the sustainability of housing projects?
- What appear to be the principal constraints in implementing measures to assess the sustainability of residential developments in the UK?
- To what extent are sustainable construction practices being used on housing development projects?

- To what extent are developers considering 'sustainability' in the development process, and how well understood is it as a concept?
- What are the main drivers and barriers to adopting sustainable construction methods on housing developments?
- How are developers approaching decisions between redevelopment and refurbishment options?

7.2 METHODOLOGY

The composition of and response to the national postal survey, sent to 2,767 addresses, is summarised in Table 7.1. One reminder letter was issued to boost the response rate.

An important consideration for the research was that all respondents should be involved in housing development (new build and/or refurbishment), in order for the survey to be able to obtain information about their decision-making strategies. Of the total number of respondents (343, a response rate of 12.4%), the respondents were screened to take account of those involved in residential schemes, and 218 respondents fell into this category, giving a valid response of 7.9%. The distribution of responses, across house builders and professional advisers, is shown in Table 7.2.

Table 7.1: Survey response rate

Respondents	Questionnaires sent	Total received	Number of respondents as a percentage of total questionnaires sent to their group	Number of respondents as a percentage of total questionnaires sent
House builders	802	104	13.0%	3.8%
Architects	487	52	10.7%	1.9%
Building surveyors	508	60	11.8%	2.2%
Housing associations	474	46	9.7%	1.7%
Quantity surveyors	496	81	16.3%	2.9%
Total	2,767	343	12.4%	12.4%

Table 7.2: Respondents involved in housing development

Respondents	Involved in housing projects (valid response)	Not involved in housing projects
House builders	87	18
Architects	38	13
Building surveyors	35	26
Housing associations	14	31
Quantity surveyors	44	37
Total	218	125

7.3   THE SURVEY FINDINGS

7.3.1 Respondents' involvement in housing development

Of the 218 respondents, 40% worked for private housing developers, 10% for social housing developers, and 50% for professional consultancy firms. Their job roles are illustrated in Figure 7.1, which shows that of the 37% holding management positions (managing director, development director, director and manager) most (62%) were employed by private housing developers. Amongst the professional advisers (project managers, surveyors and architects) most worked for independent consultancy firms (79%), although a few were directly employed by private or social house builders. Buyers (8% of respondents) were mostly employed by private house builders, although a few worked in the social sector.

Most respondents worked solely on private housing schemes (44%) or on both private and social schemes (47%), rather than on social housing only (9%) (see Figure 7.2). Professional advisers were more likely to have experience of both private and social schemes (54%).

Most respondents also worked on both new build and refurbished housing (42%) or new build only (38%), rather than specialising in refurbishment (11%) (see Figure 7.3). Of the private developers, most worked on new-build housing only (64%), whereas more professional advisers (50%) and social housing providers (54%) had experience of both new build and refurbishment projects.

Respondents were asked whether the volume of refurbishment they were involved in had changed in the last five years. Of the 114 respondents that worked on refurbishment projects, 39% said the amount

Key for figures 7.1 to 7.3

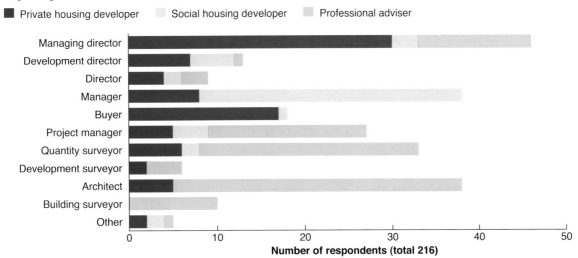

Figure 7.1: Respondents' job roles

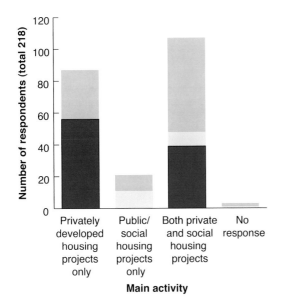

Figure 7.2: Respondents' involvement in private and social housing projects

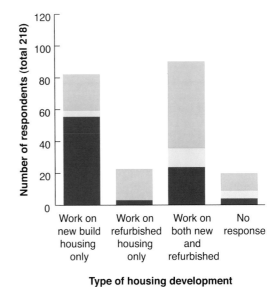

Figure 7.3: Respondents' involvement in new build housing and refurbishment

of refurbishment has stayed the same, 42% said it had increased, and 17% said it had decreased (see Figure 7.4).

The scale of respondents' involvement in housing development is illustrated in Figures 7.5 and 7.6, according to the number of completions in their last financial year. This shows that the greatest activity, with completions of over 100 units and up to 2,000 units, was amongst private developers (48%) and social housing developers (47%), whereas professional advisers (81%) were more likely to be involved in 100 units or fewer completions. Respondents specialising in new-build housing were more likely to work on large schemes, whereas those working on refurbishment projects tended to work on smaller schemes.

In terms of geographical distribution, respondents' regional operations are highly concentrated in the South East (30%) and the Greater London area (22%), followed closely by the South West region (22%) (see Figure 7.7).

Most survey respondents had not been involved in conservation-led regeneration projects (69%) or HMR projects (77%) (see Table 7.3). Of the respondents that had worked on conservation-led renewal projects (65, or 30%), most (63%) were professional advisers, followed by private housing developers (28%). Involvement in housing market renewal projects (19%) was almost evenly represented by private housing developers (36%), social housing developers (28%) and professional advisers (36%).

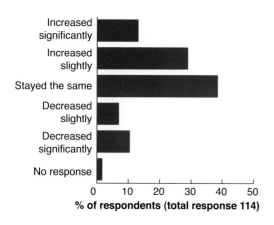

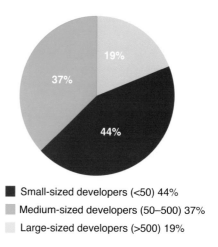

Figure 7.4: Respondents' view of the change in housing refurbishment in the last five years

Figure 7.6: Size of housing projects respondents worked on (by number of units)

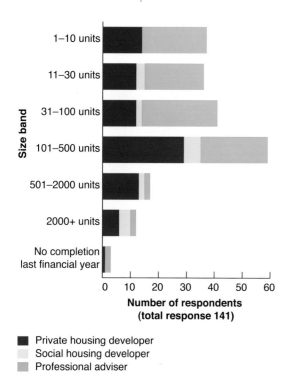

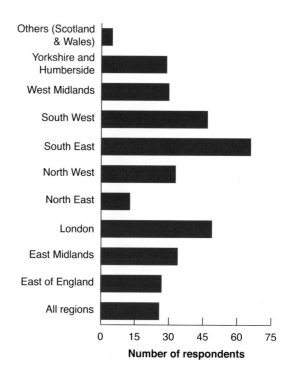

Figure 7.5: Respondents' involvement in housing development according to number of units completed in their last financial year

Figure 7.7: Respondents by region of activity years

Table 7.3: Respondents' involvement in conservation-led regeneration and housing market renewal projects

	Have you been involved in conservation-led regeneration projects?	Have you been involved in housing market renewal regeneration projects?
No	150 (69%)	167 (77%)
Yes	65 (30%)	42 (19%)
No response	3 (1%)	9 (4%)
Total	218	218

7.3.2 Measuring sustainability and environmental standards

Monitoring sustainability of housing projects was 'always' undertaken by 20% of respondents and 'sometimes' by 41%, but 39% either never undertook monitoring (21%), did not know whether the schemes they worked on were monitored (14%), or did not respond to this question (3%) (see Figure 7.8). A higher proportion of social housing providers 'always' or 'sometimes' monitored sustainability of housing projects (86%) than private housing developers (60%) or professional advisers (58%).

Overall, respondents involved in a larger number of housing completions were more likely to monitor sustainability: monitoring was 'always' undertaken by 31% of those involved in a large number of completions in the last financial year (over 500), 24% of those in the medium category (51–500 completions) and 19% in the 'small category' (under 50 completions).

The survey results also indicated that well-established measurement tools, such as EcoHomes and SAP ratings, were more commonly used than measures that had been more recently introduced (see Figure 7.9). SAP ratings in particular were 'always' used by 49% of all respondents and by 59% of private developers. The EcoHomes rating was 'always' used by 19% of respondents.

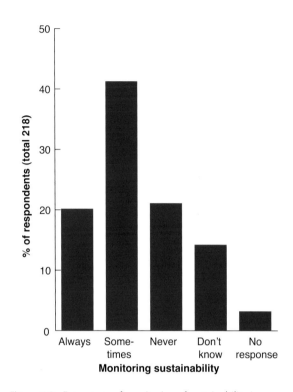

Figure 7.8: Frequency of monitoring of sustainability in residential projects

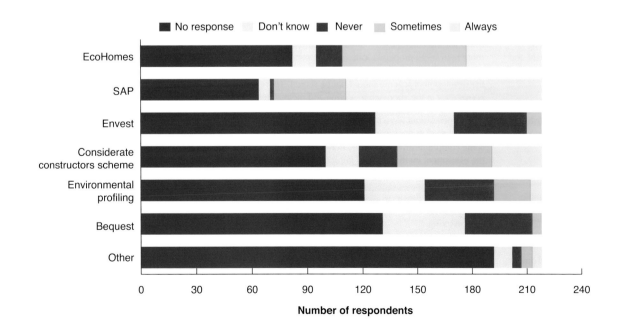

Figure 7.9: Survey of respondents' use of codes for assessing sustainability

7.3.4 The redevelopment versus refurbishment debate

Respondents were asked about the factors that they believed were important in influencing decisions about demolishing older housing in favour of redevelopment (Figure 7.14).

Based on the average score (and rated as important or very important by over 60% of respondents), the top three factors were:

* the fact that there is no VAT on new build;
* the ability to achieve more modern scheme layouts; and
* lower construction costs.

Respondents specialising in new-build housing projects tended to rate all the factors as more important than did those involved in refurbishment.

Respondent were also asked what factors they believed were most important in decisions to refurbish older housing rather than demolish and rebuild. Based on the average scores of importance (see Figure 7.15), the top three factors were:

* heritage conservation;
* retention of communities; and
* satisfaction of market demand.

Respondents involved in refurbishment tended to place greater importance on these factors than those involved in new-build development only. The opportunity to save 'embodied' energy ranked as least important, except amongst respondents engaged solely in refurbishment projects.

Respondents were then asked about the extent to which they agreed with a series of statements concerning issues of refurbishment, sustainability and energy conservation. The results are illustrated in Figure 7.16.

Key for Figures 7.14 to 7.16

■ Work on new build and refurbishment ▨ Work on refurbishment only ▨ Work on new build only

Average score (1= Not important 5 = Very important)

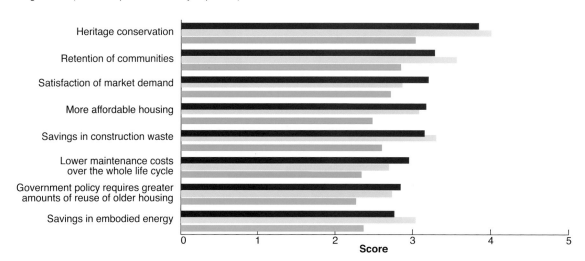

Figure 7.14: Factors important in influencing decisions to refurbish older housing rather than demolish

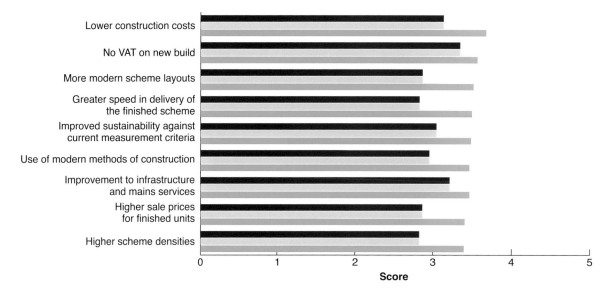

Figure 7.15: Factors important in decisions to demolish older housing in favour of new development

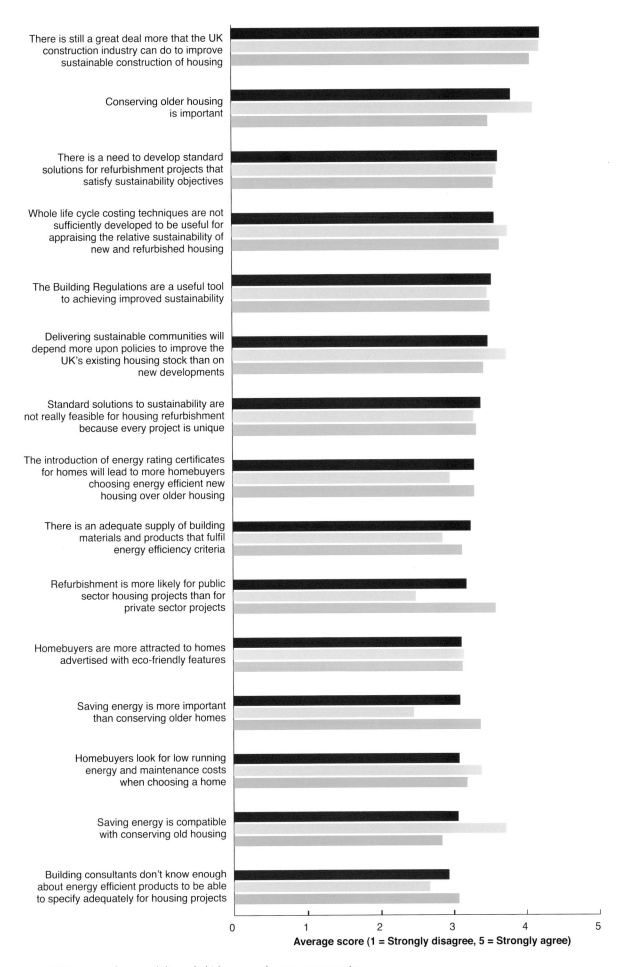

Figure 7.16: Issues of sustainability, refurbishment and energy conservation

Overall, 86% of respondents agreed or strongly agreed that "there is still a great deal that the UK construction industry can do to improve the sustainable construction of housing".

There was also relatively strong agreement that "conserving older housing is important" (66% agreed or strongly agreed), especially amongst respondents involved in refurbishment, but less agreement that "saving energy is more important than conserving older homes" (37%) or that "saving energy is compatible with conserving older housing" (34%). Respondents specialising in new housing were more inclined to the idea that saving energy is more important than and less compatible with building conservation. The idea that eco-friendly features and low annual running costs influenced homebuyers also scored relatively low. In the comments section of the questionnaire respondents also indicated that refurbished property could satisfy a current strong market for historic or period property, and where "the design quality of older homes is often more attractive to a client, this often comes before any desire to reduce energy costs".

Somewhat contradictory evidence also emerged, because although 62% agreed or strongly agreed that "there is a need to develop standard solutions for refurbishment projects that satisfy sustainability objectives", there was also relatively strong opinion (amongst 50%) that "standard solutions to sustainability are not really feasible for housing refurbishment because every project is unique". Whole-life costing techniques were also generally viewed as "not sufficiently well developed to be useful for appraising the relative sustainability of new and refurbished housing".

On questions concerning the effectiveness of the Building Regulations in promoting sustainable construction (also see Figures 7.17 and 7.18, 59% of respondents agreed or strongly agreed that the Building Regulations were a useful tool in this regard, particularly for new housing (85%) rather than refurbished housing. Respondents involved in new housing development were also more inclined to agree (than those working on refurbishment projects) that the Building Regulations are less effective than market demand in influencing

Key for Figures 7.17 to 7.19

■ Work on new build and refurbishment ■ Work on refurbishment only ■ Work on new build only

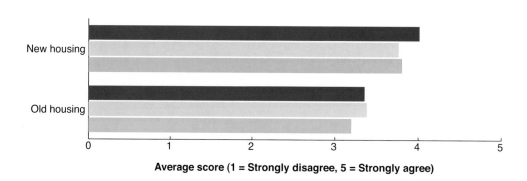

Figure 7.17: Part L of the Building Regulations is an effective measure for improving the energy efficiency of new housing and/or refurbished housing

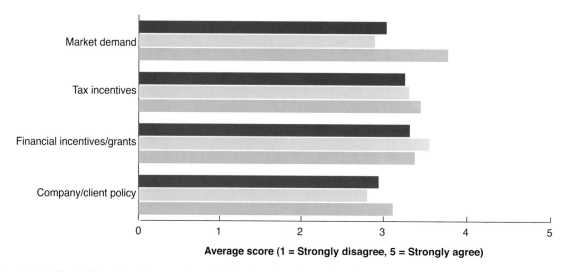

Figure 7.18: The Building Regulations are less effective than these factors for achieving improved sustainability

sustainable practices, whereas respondents working on refurbishment projects tended to favour tax and financial incentives and grants. This would suggest that although respondents generally appeared to believe that eco-friendly and energy efficiency features are not currently a significant factor affecting homebuyer choices, a change in consumer attitudes could do more than regulation to influence sustainable building practices, particularly amongst developers of new housing.

On government policy generally, 50% of respondents agreed or strongly agreed that "*delivering sustainable communities will depend more upon policies to improve the UK's existing housing stock than on new developments*". However, most respondents were neutral or disagreed that the "*housing market renewal scheme is well understood by private housing developers*" (79%) or that the policy was "*likely to succeed in creating sustainable housing*" (75%). More respondents agreed or strongly agreed that social housing developers understood this policy (47%). See Figure 7.19.

Respondents were asked in free-format questions for their views about what they saw as the single biggest incentive and drawback to housing refurbishment over demolition and redevelopment. Analysis of the responses is summarised in Table 7.5.

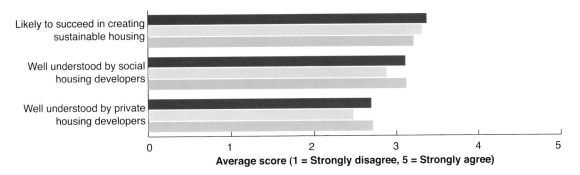

Figure 7.19: The housing market renewal scheme

Table 7.5: Incentives versus drawbacks to refurbishing older housing

Biggest incentives (169 respondents, 77%)	Biggest drawbacks (189 respondents, 82%)
Cost/financial savings (32%) – Upfront costs for site acquisition can be lower, as can costs of building work per units, making refurbishment projects cost effective with good financial returns.	Cost and complexity (51%) – Costs per m² can be higher compared with new builds. There is also greater cost uncertainty with refurbishment due to 'hidden' or unexpected costs that could not be predicted or planned for at the project feasibility stage. Refurbishment is therefore more 'risky'.
Retention of established environmental character/ communities (23%) – There is value in retaining the existing character and environmental features of an area. Refurbishment can also help to maintain communities and encourage the conservation of architectural heritage.	Standards/quality (18%) – The quality of a refurbished building is not as good as a new building because the basic structure is still old and probably near the end of its serviceable life. The reuse of old buildings also means that standards expected of new buildings cannot be met, for example, in terms of energy efficiency,
Suitable stock for refurbishment (8%) – When the character of buildings and their surrounding environment is attractive and contributes to the sense of identity in an area, then they are worthy of retention.	Land use and design – Old buildings can also be inflexible in terms of achieving room layouts to meet modern living requirements.
Architectural/planning considerations (10%) – When buildings have been 'listed' in order to ensure retention of attractive architectural features demolition is generally not an option. From the planning procedural side, developers willing to refurbish a listed building face fewer barriers and applications tend to undergo a quicker planning process.	Construction issues (8%) – The construction process for a refurbishment can be more complex. Alterations and adaptation of old buildings are not always straightforward, for example where there is the need for underpinning. There are more time delays involved with refurbishment projects at all stages, including tender, procurement and construction. There is a lack of skills within the building industry, with a particular shortage of experience in refurbishment work.
Speed (7%) – For simple conversions, refurbishment can be easier and quicker.	
VAT (5%) – Where the refurbishment achieves energy rating/targets that attract tax relief, particularly VAT zero rating, they can be attractive.	VAT (8%) – VAT on the alteration of existing buildings makes the cost differential with new build too great, favouring new build. VAT should therefore be zero rated on refurbishment where the end product is residential units.
Market demand (5%) – When the nature of the finished refurbished homes attracts prospective purchasers, as one respondent pointed out, 'the design quality of older homes is often more attractive to a client, this often comes before any desire to reduce energy costs'.	Community issues (5%) – Refurbishment of houses cannot necessarily overcome problems in communities characterised by social problems, difficulties with tenanted property, poor design, lack of green spaces and poor infrastructure.
Sustainable construction (4%) – Refurbishment assists waste reduction of material leaving the site because there is no demolition involved.	Planning and density (6%) – Meeting planning requirements for refurbishment is more difficult because of additional constraints, especially in conservation areas. Refurbishment also limits the housing density to that existing.

Figures 7.20 and 7.21 compare respondents' comments between those whose work involved refurbishment projects and those that worked on new-build housing.

Overall there was a slightly lower response on the issue of incentives (77%) as compared with drawbacks (82%).

The biggest incentives to refurbishment identified by most respondents were cost and financial savings (32%), followed by the opportunity to retain established environmental character and communities (23%), particularly mentioned by respondents that specialised in refurbishment (33%). A suitable stock of attractive buildings encourages refurbishment (8%) and a willingness to refurbish buildings that are listed can result in a quicker planning process (10%). For simple conversions, refurbishment can also be easier and quicker (7%), whereas more major refurbishments that attract VAT zero rating

or tax relief, through achieving energy rating targets, can also be attractive (5%). Market demand for refurbished homes can be strong where the design quality is good, outweighing considerations of energy efficiency (5%). Sustainable construction and the opportunity to save on demolition waste was the least-mentioned factor (4%).

The biggest drawbacks to refurbishment over demolition and new build mentioned by most respondents were cost and complexity (51%), followed by difficulties in meeting standards or quality for finished homes (18%). Respondents who specialised in new-build projects particularly perceived cost as a drawback (66%), whereas standards were of more concern to those specialising in refurbishment (33%) and to social housing developers (26%). Refurbishment is more risky because the extent of the work needed on buildings is not always fully uncovered until a start has been made on site: therefore hidden or unexpected

Key for Figures 7.20 and 7.21

■ Work on new build and refurbishment   ■ Work on refurbishment only   ■ Work on new build only

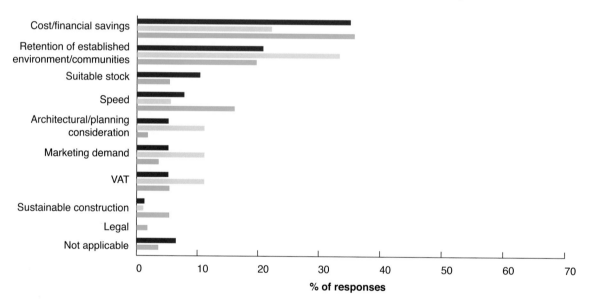

Figure 7.20: Biggest incentive to housing refurbishment rather than new build

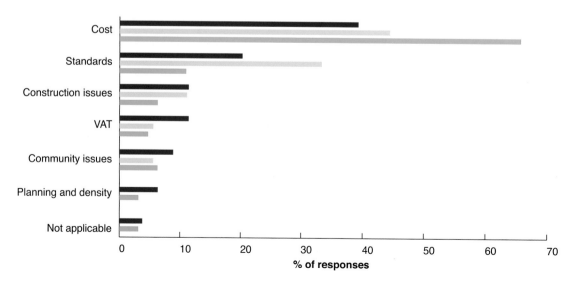

Figure 7.21: Biggest single drawback to housing refurbishment over new build

costs can arise that were not planned for at the project feasibility stage. The construction process is therefore more complex and prone to time delays (8%). VAT also makes the cost differential against new build too great (8%). Refurbishment will also not necessarily overcome problems in communities characterised by social problems, tenant resistance to change, poor design and lack of infrastructure (5%), particularly identified by social housing developers (16%). Meeting planning requirements can also be more difficult, particularly in conservation areas, and housing density is limited by the existing layout (6%).

7.3.5 Improving sustainable construction

The final question in the survey gave respondents the opportunity to comment in their own words on what they saw as being needed to improve the sustainable construction of housing in the UK, and 149 (68%) completed this question. The factors they identified are summarised in Figure 7.22. The top five were:

- financial incentives, including VAT equalisation (38%);
- tighter/universal regulation, including Building Regulations and planning (24%);
- raising understanding, knowledge and education (19%);
- a more positive planning environment (15%); and
- simplified and standardised guidance (15%).

7.3.5.1   Financial incentives

Respondents recommended a range of financial incentives aimed at the development industry, homeowners and tenants, including:

- financial encouragement to save and recycle demolition waste;
- grants towards housing refurbishment projects, the use of energy-efficient features and sustainable construction techniques;

- equalising VAT on refurbishment and new-build projects;
- stamp duty and council tax reductions for purchasers and occupiers of greener homes; and
- grants for first-time buyers to improve existing homes;

It was emphasised by survey respondents that developments have to be economically viable, and that house builders cannot afford to and will not participate in projects that are likely to result in a financial loss. Refurbishment is generally more risky than new build, particularly for property in relatively poor condition, and central government initiatives are seen as crucial to the creation of confidence and risk reduction, attracting investment into refurbishing the existing housing stock.

A big concern amongst respondents was the current discrepancy between the levels of VAT charged on new build and refurbishment (see Section 5.4). Many practitioners recommended that to encourage refurbishment VAT should the same as for new-build projects, to create a 'level playing field'.

The introduction of financial incentives for achieving sustainability or penalties for failing to meet basic sustainability criteria was also suggested to address the quality and design of UK homes. Financial grants towards the use of new technology and MMC are particularly needed to *"enable demand to push down high initial costs and provide economies of scale"*. Although market forces are expected to drive developers towards greater sustainability, it is still more expensive to build a sustainable house than to use conventional construction, and although costs are likely to reduce over time *"this seems to be some way off yet"*. Therefore, as one respondent commented:

"The costs of sustainable materials must be kept competitive, particularly in the private housing sector... it must be remembered that all developers are only building to make a profit."

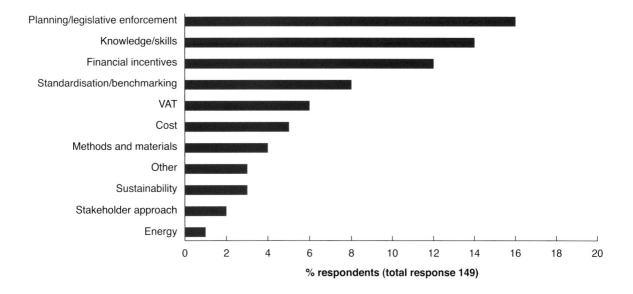

Figure 7.22: Areas of concern regarding government policy

7.3.5.2 Tighter regulation

Respondents expressed the view that if sustainable homes are to be delivered then construction standards must be set by government through legislation, and should be:

- applied universally to private and social housing;
- sufficiently flexible to be capable of application in a range of situations, particularly in refurbishment projects, where the base structure and local environment can vary considerably;
- sufficiently robust to be enforceable; and
- applied consistently and actively enforced throughout the regulatory process, including Building Regulations, planning conditions and codes for measuring/monitoring sustainability.

This is needed because:

"Only legislation provides a level playing field by which all comply and thus creates even competition for the new house buyer."

"Private house builders need to [be subject to] the same rules, regulations and requirements as affordable house providers."

"House builders will always seek the cheapest way to construct houses. Their methods change only when forced to by regulation."

7.3.5.3 Understanding, knowledge and education

Respondents identified a need to raise understanding, improve knowledge and widen education about housing sustainability amongst all stakeholders in the development process, including house builders, their advisers, planners, construction workers, local communities and householders, particularly homebuyers.

Several developers felt that raising knowledge and understanding about sustainability issues would facilitate greater efficiency in decision-making processes and improve communication between the many professional disciplines and other stakeholders involved in housing development.

Construction professionals in particular needed more information about:

- the use of MMC, including ways to achieve cost benefits from adopting new methods;
- the availability and use of sustainable building materials; and
- methods for assessing environmental impact.

As one developer stated:

"… knowledge of best practice and an insistence on whole-life costing in the planning process is required, together with improved awareness of materials and grants to 'force the change'."

7.3.5.4 A more positive planning environment

Respondents felt that the practical effects of the new emphasis on sustainable construction had not been fully recognised by local planning authorities. A more imaginative and positive approach was needed to resolve issues around:

- planners' resistance to the use of new and alternative materials in house construction that are designed to meet sustainability criteria;
- planners' failure to understand market demand and consumer attitudes in terms of the marketability of finished homes; and
- conflicts between using new construction methods and achieving housing diversity.

As developers commented:

"The government needs to … reconcile some of the conflicting policies, such as the drive for 'off site' solutions and the planners' insistence on diversity with project house-type mix."

"Planning needs to reflect medium-term local demand for housing types and numbers. One drive over the last few years has been to maximise densities through PPS3…this has led to too many apartments being built … this is not sustainable in the medium or long term."

7.3.5.5 Simplified and standardised guidance

Respondents called for greater simplification and standardisation of the various codes now in use for measuring sustainable construction, such as EcoHomes, SAP ratings and BREEAM. The codes are not always easy to interpret, particularly in relation to refurbishment projects, and:

"… the current 'make it up as we go' evolvement of eco-ratings, building regulations (and others) is not conducive to swift delivery of consistently higher standards of homes."

"The government needs to legislate, but with a simple process for measurement and needs to reconcile some of the conflicting policies …"

Survey respondents also directed a degree of criticism towards the implementation of the new Part L standard, particularly related to its timetable. Several practitioners felt that it had come out too quickly for a full understanding of its key objectives. One respondent summed this up, stating that *"there needs to be some time for us all to understand the new Part L building regulations…".*

Standards also needed to be recognised by homebuyers:

"In my opinion, sustainable housing will only be recognised by the buying public if government regulations enforce some type of benchmarking regime, thus allowing consumers to rate developers/developments on a 'sustainability' score."

7.4 SUMMARY

The survey findings are summarised in relation to the following key themes:

- the redevelopment versus refurbishment debate;
- the use of sustainable construction techniques;
- measuring sustainable development and construction; and
- ways to improve housing sustainability in the UK.

7.4.1 The redevelopment versus refurbishment debate

The survey indicates that, overall, respondents see more drawbacks than incentives to housing refurbishment over demolition and new build. However, of the respondents that worked on refurbishment projects, most considered that the level of refurbishment had stayed the same or increased over the last five years, with less than one fifth observing that the level had decreased.

Refurbishment can work under certain conditions, where the original stock is in reasonable condition and has attractive features worthy of retention that will attract market demand. Projects can also be cost-effective where the stock is capable of relatively simple, quick conversion, or on more major projects that attract VAT zero rating or tax relief. Respondents working on refurbishment also tend to be involved in smaller projects than those working on new-build housing schemes.

Respondents recognised that refurbishing existing stock offered the following advantages:

- contribution to heritage conservation;
- contribution towards the retention of existing communities; and
- an opportunity to satisfy market demand.

Nevertheless, refurbishment is more risky and costly where the existing stock is in poor condition. The physical problems of old structures are not always readily apparent before starting the refurbishment work, and it is not easy to meet the standards expected of new developments in terms of energy efficiency, room layouts and design. Although the benefits of retaining the existing environmental character and communities are recognised, refurbishment cannot necessarily overcome community problems associated with social issues, tenant resistance, poor design and lack of infrastructure. Respondents' reasons for preferring new build to refurbishment projects are therefore as follows:

- reduced risk and uncertainty;
- elimination of VAT;
- lower construction cost;
- higher scheme densities; and
- more modern scheme layouts.

All of these factors are seen as contributing towards the profitability of a scheme. Respondents that specialise in new-build housing weighted the advantages of new build more strongly than those that work on refurbishment projects, and are particularly more inclined to the view that saving energy is more important than and less compatible with building conservation.

Attitudes to refurbishment therefore appear to vary based on respondents' experience – that is, whether they have been involved in refurbishment projects or specialise in new-build housing. Decisions about redevelopment versus refurbishment on specific sites could therefore be influenced by the experience and specialisation of the prospective developers and their professional advisers, rather than being based purely on a site appraisal, particularly in the absence of well-developed appraisal techniques to enable valid comparisons.

7.4.2 Measuring sustainable development and construction

In terms of appraising the relative sustainability of new-build and refurbished housing projects, the SAP, EcoHomes and whole life costing approaches were not rated very highly, and most respondents agreed that whole life cycle costing techniques are currently not sufficiently well developed to be useful in this context.

The well-established measurement tools, such as EcoHomes and SAP ratings, are more commonly used for measuring environmental performance of residential development schemes than measures that have been more recently introduced. Monitoring is also more commonly undertaken by social housing providers than by private housing developers, and is more likely to be used on larger schemes.

The following suggestions were made for the improvement of assessment methods:

- making the assessment criteria more applicable, relevant and consistent;
- creating a single system/monitoring body; and
- making the process easier/simpler.

Most respondents believed that the Building Regulations could be used to achieve greater levels of sustainable construction. However, respondents criticised the 'tinkering' approach by government to such fundamental guidance as the Building Regulations, and the absence of appropriate coherent guidance, which acted as a barrier to implementation.

Somewhat contradictory evidence also emerged, because while most respondents said that there is a need to develop standard solutions for refurbishment projects that satisfy sustainability objectives, about half of the respondents thought that standard solutions are not really appropriate for refurbishments because every project is unique.

7.4.3 Use of sustainable construction techniques

There is evidence of the use of MMC, with timber frame being the most popular, and with one third of respondents using prefabricated components, used most by respondents specialising in new-build projects. Of the bespoke measures incorporated into residential schemes, the most popular were the use of water recycling facilities, solar water heating and sustainable wood burning.

Less than half the respondents had formal construction and demolition (C&D) waste management processes for housing projects, and these are more likely on new build than on refurbishments. Of the minority who had a formal policy on the reuse of materials for the schemes they worked on, most were involved in refurbishment projects, particularly conservation-led refurbishment.

While respondents generally appeared to believe that eco-friendly and energy efficient features are not currently a strong influence on homebuyer choices, they also believed that a change in consumer attitudes could do more than regulation to encourage sustainable construction practices, particularly for new housing.

Overall, respondents recognised that the construction industry can do a great deal more to improve sustainable construction.

7.4.4 Improving housing sustainability

In terms of improving housing sustainability in the UK, respondents laid particular emphasis on the need for:

- financial incentives, including VAT equalisation, to encourage the use of sustainable construction practices and the refurbishment of existing housing;
- tighter/universal regulation of construction standards, including consistent application and active enforcement of Building Regulations and planning conditions;
- raising understanding, knowledge and education across the development sector, including house builders, professional advisers, planners, construction workers and householders, particularly homebuyers;
- a more positive planning environment, which embraces the use of new and more sustainable construction practices toward the delivery of homes that people want; and
- simplified and standardised guidance.

8 CONCLUSIONS AND FURTHER RESEARCH

8.1 INTRODUCTION

The overall aim of this research is to assess the sustainability of newly constructed housing, in comparison with the refurbishment of existing housing, in the context of the government's SCP.

The objectives of the research are as follows:

1. to assess the construction sector's attitudes to the sustainability of refurbishing older housing versus demolition and new build;

2. to examine the range of methodologies (including whole life cycle costing) available to house builders to assess the relative sustainability of housing construction and refurbishment;

3. to examine the methods actually used by house builders to evaluate the relative sustainability of new-build housing versus refurbishment;

4. to investigate the main drivers and barriers towards housing construction and refurbishment;

5. to review the sustainable construction techniques being employed by house builders.

8.2 METHODOLOGY

The research aims and objectives were achieved through a literature review and questionnaire survey.

Literature and policy review. A desktop review was undertaken of the literature/policy guidance and previous research relating to construction and refurbishment of housing, with a particular emphasis on economic/WLCA.

National survey. A national survey of house builders, quantity surveyors, development surveyors and architects was conducted to assess attitudes and perceptions towards sustainable construction; MMC; existing standards of sustainability; and the use of sustainability assessment tool kits.

8.3 RESEARCH RESULTS

The results of the literature review and the outcome of the national survey are considered in the light of two main government policies. First, the SCP proposes a long-term strategy for delivering sustainable communities in both urban and rural areas. This goal is to be achieved in part by tackling the problems of low demand and abandonment of housing experienced in parts of the Midlands and North of England by the establishment of HMR pathfinder areas.

The problems of low demand and abandonment of housing are, however, not caused entirely by poor-quality housing alone, it seems. The literature discusses a wide range of social problems that either contribute to the unpopularity of areas of abandoned housing or which, if caused by poor housing initially, are a major factor contributing to the downward spiral of some inner cities. These create a contagion effect, like a 'virus', which can lead to whole neighbourhoods becoming devoid of social and economic activity. The extent to which housing renewal (using either refurbishment or demolition and new-build policies) can reverse such widespread social and environmental problems is not yet clear.

8.3.1 Objectives 1 and 4

Sustainability of refurbishing older housing versus demolition and new build: drivers and barriers
Despite the government's SCP, within which the pathfinder areas have been established, there has been widespread criticism that the policies that have been adopted are not in fact sustainable; that they are wasteful not only of energy and of the heritage value of the dwellings that, in some locations, are being demolished and replaced, but also of the social value inherent in keeping existing communities together. Lessons do not seem to have been learned from the failed policies of mass clearance adopted in the 1960s and 1970s, and there is concern that the replacement dwellings will be as physically and socially (and therefore economically) unsustainable as the accommodation constructed to replace the dwellings demolished in the previous century.

Organisations such as English Heritage and CABE have called for recognition of the heritage value of pre-1919 Victorian dwellings, and for refurbishment (rather than demolition) to be the preferred option. There are a whole range of arguments to support the sustainability of this policy, including their heritage value, the retention of their embodied energy, and the fact that refurbishment is far less expensive, in both financial and energy terms. Generally this policy seems to receive the support of local communities.

However, in areas of low demand and abandonment it may be that there is no demand at all for any form of residential accommodation, of whatever design, quality or price. There is evidence from the literature, for example, that even newly built dwellings are standing empty, having never been occupied. English Heritage recognises that it may not always be appropriate to replace demolished dwellings.

The results of the national survey demonstrate that there is widespread recognition within the industry of the advantages (at least in sustainability terms) of refurbishment. Thus refurbishment is seen as an opportunity to supply more affordable housing: it generates less waste, and it contributes towards heritage conservation as well as to the retention of existing communities. There is no evidence that the industry is incapable of undertaking refurbishment work, since a relatively high proportion of the respondents have been involved in refurbishment work.

Despite these advantages, the research has demonstrated a range of perceived barriers to refurbishment. There was contradictory evidence as to the relative costs of refurbishment compared with new build, with the greater proportion of the respondents viewing new build as cheaper on a unit (per square metre) basis. It is not possible to get away from the fact that a refurbished building has an inherently old structure, which by implication shortens its future useful life. There is also the perception that certain modern standards, eg in terms of energy efficiency and configuration, could not be met within a refurbished dwelling. Refurbishment is seen as the more complex option, with planning policies (especially within conservation areas) an additional constraint. There is also a perception that refurbishment tends to be undertaken in 'poor' locations that have poor infrastructure, which has implications both for the refurbishment process and for the resale opportunities of the completed dwellings. Additionally, given the disadvantage of full rate VAT (compared with new build, which is zero rated), and the lack of skills for refurbishing older dwellings sympathetically within the building industry, it is clear that new build is the more attractive choice.

Given the profit motive underpinning both the construction industry and the drive of market forces for housing accommodation, without a clear price advantage the other benefits associated with new build are likely to sway both builders and the public against the more sustainable option. What is also of concern is the perception that the public does not value eco-friendly dwellings. Whether or not this perception reflects the reality of the marketplace, for as long as the industry believes that there is no price advantage in eco-friendly housing, then such dwellings are unlikely to be provided as standard unless there is clear and specific government direction.

It is therefore unsurprising that there is a clear preference for demolition and rebuild, both in the achievements of the pathfinder schemes to date and in the responses to the national survey. New-build schemes are seen as meeting the needs of the marketplace better. There is no constraint imposed by existing buildings on the size, configuration, layout and amenities within the immediate locality, as there is with refurbishment. The chance to offer 'new' accommodation to the marketplace, which reflects fashionable values and is constructed of modern materials, increases the certainty of product outcomes and allows for the achievement of qualities such as cost certainty and a reduction of risk in management. Thus demolition and rebuild offers a chance to develop a cleared site, with all the flexibility of planning, design, layout and densities that go with it. There is also the perception that new build is what the market wants, and given the fact that the construction industry is profit-driven, the preference for new build is entirely logical.

8.3.2 Objectives 2 and 3

The range of methodologies (including whole life cycle costing) available to house builders to assess the relative sustainability of housing construction and refurbishment, and the methods actually used by house builders to evaluate the relative sustainability of new-build housing versus refurbishment

There is evidence that decisions about whether to demolish and rebuild or whether to refurbish an existing dwelling are based, at least in part, on cost, whether that be in financial or environmental terms. However, there is a tendency to compare initial costs only. It is increasingly recognised that most of the CO_2 emissions from housing result not from the initial construction period (although that activity generates a large amount of greenhouse gas) but from the subsequent period of occupation. Increasing attention is now being paid to some form of LCCA, although more so by professional advisers than by builders, when designing and constructing dwellings, so that an early evaluation can result in long-term reductions of CO_2 emissions, reduced occupation costs and increased energy efficiency.

Section 6 of this report evaluates the range of methodologies available to the industry, although it is clear from the survey that it is mainly the larger house builders who more commonly monitor the sustainability of their residential schemes; a large proportion had either never monitored their schemes or considered that monitoring was not important. A range of monitoring schemes was reviewed, some of which appear highly complex, and few of which are recognised within the regulatory framework. There is also evidence that the tools used in the UK to monitor schemes are based on different principles from those used elsewhere, which makes international comparison of the sustainability of construction inappropriate.

Despite the range of assessment methods available, respondents seemed unclear about how to use these tools, and considered that a reliable assessment mechanism is lacking. The most popular assessment tools were the 'traditional' mechanisms of EcoHomes and SAP ratings. The apparent popularity of these tools may result from the lead taken by local planning authorities, which can require that schemes meet specified targets.

There is evidence from the literature of the unreliability of SAP ratings (for example) when measuring carbon emissions, and also a perception that life cycle costing techniques are not sufficiently well developed to be useful for appraising the relative sustainability of schemes.

Respondents to the study suggested that assessment mechanisms would benefit from increased consistency of approach, scoring and measurement; and that the process of calculation and the methodologies used should be simpler.

8.3.3 Objective 5

Review the sustainable construction techniques being employed by house builders
It is generally recognised that traditional methods of construction (using bricks and mortar) are highly unsustainable, for example in terms of the unnecessary energy used and the waste generated. There is also a skills shortage within the construction industry, which means that some work is not undertaken by experienced experts, with a resulting poor quality of output. Skills shortage is particularly prevalent for the refurbishment of Victorian heritage buildings, and puts the inherent aesthetic value of the structure at risk if remedial work is not undertaken sympathetically and appropriately.

The advantages offered by MMC, with standardised factory processes for producing units for site assembly, which result in 'deskilling' of the process, were well recognised by the respondents in the survey. A significant proportion of the respondents use timber frame construction, largely on new-build projects, and there is evidence of the use of prefabricated components, steel frame and concrete frames for residential developments.

The survey did not investigate the extent to which such alternative forms of construction are, or are seen to be, more sustainable than traditional methodologies. However, they have clear advantages for contractors in terms of the time saved in the construction process.

8.3.4 The overall aim

To assess the sustainability of newly constructed housing, in comparison with the refurbishment of existing housing, in the context of the government's Sustainable Communities Plan
The research has investigated the relative sustainability of newly constructed housing in comparison with the refurbishment of existing housing, in the light of the government's SCP. Particular emphasis has been placed on the dilemma facing those responsible for the pathfinder areas, in the light of widespread criticisms. The concern is that a large amount of pre-1919 Victorian

housing has heritage value, and should be retained and refurbished for the benefit of future generations.

Such a retention policy also supports principles of sustainability in terms of the retention of embodied energy, reduced waste within the refurbishment process (compared to demolition and new build), a shorter (re)construction period, and, it can be argued, lower costs.

However, there are barriers to such a policy, not the least of which is the apparent preference of the construction industry for new build (see Section 8.3.1 above). If the sustainable option of refurbishment is to become more attractive, then a range of measures need to be taken. These are outlined below (Section 8.4).

8.4 RESEARCH RECOMMENDATIONS

Based on the national survey undertaken for this research, the recommendations focus on the need for clarity, consistency and financial incentives to support both sustainable construction in general and refurbishment of existing dwellings in particular. Thus:

- Clear guidelines are needed on what 'sustainability' means for the construction industry.
- Government should consider financial inducement for refurbishment projects in order to make them economically viable and more attractive when compared with demolition and new build, including:
  - tax breaks;
  - financial rewards for the reuse of materials;
  - financial rewards for the use of a formalised waste management strategy;
  - at least a 'level playing field' for new build and refurbishment (if not a positive advantage for refurbishment) within the VAT regime;
  - a review of the apparent policy of local planning authorities allowing higher densities for new build;
  - sustainability criteria that demonstrate clearly the relative merits of refurbishment when compared with new build;
  - refurbishment of dwellings that is undertaken alongside improvements to local infrastructure and mains services;
  - more competitive refurbishment costs compared with new build;
  - provision of the skills necessary for sympathetic and appropriate refurbishment; and
  - planning policy and practice that is more supportive of refurbishment.
- Research should be undertaken to establish ways of using the techniques underpinning MMC within refurbishment.
- The attractions of refurbished and heritage properties should be promoted to the house-buying public.
- The benefits of sustainable features within dwellings should be promoted to the house-buying public, potentially together with recognition of the long-term advantages of a reduction of costs in use and the emission of greenhouse gases.

- Research should be undertaken to investigate whether there are any potential mechanisms within the refurbishment process that can be used to shorten the length of time involved and thereby contribute to its financial advantage.
- Greater emphasis needs to be made to reinforce both the perception and reality that refurbishment of existing dwellings saves energy in the long term.
- Monitoring of the sustainability of residential schemes should be more widely encouraged by the following:
  - easier to use and simpler methods of assessing sustainability features;
  - development and promotion of suitable and appropriate WLCA techniques to demonstrate full costs in use;
  - greater consistency in the approach to, and scoring and measurement of, assessment methodologies;
  - improved transparency in the criteria used in environmental profiling;
  - a formal network for the monitoring of assessment methods by an external organisation;
  - development of a single universal tool kit to improve understanding;
  - improved communication of assessment methodologies to stakeholders; and
  - a mandatory requirement for sustainability assessments within the planning process.

- Building Regulations should be amended so that they achieve greater sustainability.
- Research should be undertaken to ascertain how Building Regulations can be amended to achieve greater sustainability.
- Sustainability criteria for rural areas should be devised separately from those for urban areas to reflect such local issues as scarcity of resources.
- Improved communication is needed between the bodies involved, which would improve the chances of achieving sustainability.
- Greater use should be made within residential developments of such energy-saving techniques and components as:
  - formal construction and demolition waste management processes in housing projects;
  - reuse and recycling of materials within the construction industry;
  - CHP units;
  - water-recycling facilities; and
  - solar water heating.
- The industry concern regarding the inadequate supply of building materials and products which fulfil the energy efficiency criteria should be addressed.
- Greater attention needs to be paid to the minimisation of waste within the construction process.

9 REFERENCES

Alcorn A and Wood P (1998). *New Zealand Building Materials Embodied Energy Coefficients Database: Volume II Coefficients.* Victoria University of Wellington: Centre for Building Performance Research.

Anon (1998) RICS Budget Wishlist. News Release [online]. Available from: www.prnewswire.co.uk [accessed 20 March 2007].

Anon (2005). 'Sustainable Communities Will Fail' [online]. Llandysul, Carmarthenshire, Green Building Press. Available from: http://www.newbuilder.co.uk/news/NewsFullStory.asp?ID=1085 [accessed 20 March 2007].

Audit Commission (2002). *Suggested Key Indicators for Economic Regeneration.* London: HMSO.

Bagenholm C (2006). 'EcoHomes rating for refurbishment'. Paper presented at the BRE Refurb Conference, 2006, Watford.

Baker Tilly (2007). *A Guide to VAT and Property.* London: Baker Tilly.

Balsas C J L (2004). 'Measuring the livability of an urban centre: an exploratory study of key performance indicators'. *Planning, Practice & Research,* Vol. 19, No. 1, pp. 101–110.

Barker K (2003). *Review of Housing Supply: 'Securing Our Future Needs'. Interim Report – Analysis.* London: HM Treasury.

Barker K (2004). *Review of Housing Supply: 'Delivering Stability: Securing Our Future Housing Needs'. Final Report – Recommendations.* London: HM Treasury.

BCIS Online (2006). *BCIS Price Index Database* [online]. Available from: http://www.bcis.co.uk/ (subscription) [accessed: 16 June 2006].

Beacham P (2002). 'The historic environment: matrix for urban regeneration'. Paper to National Conservation Conference – *Regeneration Through Conservation.* Bristol, 24 May 2002. Unpublished.

Bell M and Lowe R (2000). 'Building regulations and sustainable housing. Part 1: A critique of Part L of the Building Regulations 1995 for England and Wales'. *Structural Survey,* Vol. 18, No. 1, pp. 28–37.

Bevan S and Dobie A (2006). 'Save our Heritage!'. *RICS Business,* February, : pp. 16–20.

Boardman B *et al.* (2005). *The 40% House.* Oxford: Oxford Environmental Change Institute, University of Oxford.

Bramley G and Pawson H (2002). 'Low demand for housing: incidence, causes and UK national policy implications'. *Urban Studies,* Vol. 39, No. 3, pp. 393–422.

British Standards Institution (1998). *Guide to the Principles of the Conservation of Historic Buildings.* BS 7913: 1998.

CABE (2003). *Building Sustainable Communities: Actions for Housing Market Renewal.* London: Commission for Architecture and the Built Environment.

Carrig Conservation (2004). *Built to Last: The Sustainable Reuse of Buildings.* Dublin: The Heritage Council and Dublin City Council.

Carter E (2006). *Making Money from Sustainable Homes: A Developer's Guide.* CIOB [online]. Available from: http://www.pdmconsultants.co.uk/filemanager/developers_guide-2.CV.pdf [accessed: 06 May 2007].

Cassar M (2006). *Sustainability and the Historic Environment.* London: Centre for Sustainable Heritage, UCL.

Chini A R and Bruening S F (2003). 'Deconstruction and materials reuse in the United States'. *The Future of Sustainable Construction,* University of Florida, 14 May 2003, pp. 1–22. www.bcn.ufl.edu/pindex/109/Chini.pdf [accessed April 2008].

CLG (2004). *What is a decent home?* [online]. Available from: www.communities.gov.uk/index.asp?id=1152146 [accessed March 2007].

CPRE (2004). *Useless Old Houses? What to Do With the North West's Low Demand Housing and High Density Heritage.* North West Regional Policy Office, Bamber Bridge, Lancashire: Council for the Preservation of Rural England.

Cullingworth J B and Nadin V (2006). *Town and Country Planning in the UK* (14th edn). London: Routledge.

DCLG (2005). *The Code for Sustainable Homes. Setting the standard in sustainability for new homes.* London: Department of Communities and Local Government.

DCLG (2006). *Review of the Sustainability of Existing Buildings: 'The Energy Efficiency of Dwellings' – Initial Analysis.* London: Department for Communities and Local Government.

DCMS and DTLR (2001). *The Historic Environment: A Force for Our Future.* London: Department for Culture, Media and Sport & Department of Transport, Local Government and the Regions.

DETR (2000a). *Local Quality of Life Counts: A Summary of a Menu of Local Indicators of Sustainable Development.* London: Department of the Environment, Transport and the Regions.

DETR (2000b). 'Regeneration that lasts: a guide to good practice on social housing estates'. In DETR (2001) *A Review of the Evidence Base for Regeneration Policy and Practice.* London: Department of the Environment, Transport and the Regions.

Dixon T, Pocock Y and Waters M (2005). *The Role of the UK Development Industry in Brownfield Regeneration: Stage 2 Report, Volume 2 (of 3): Sub-Regional Context (Thames Gateway and Greater Manchester).* Reading: The College of Estate Management.

DOE (1997). *Energy Consumption in the UK: A statistical review of delivered and primary energy consumption by sub-sector, end-use and the factors affecting change.* London: HMSO.

Drivers Jonas (2006). *Heritage Works.* London: Drivers Jonas.

DTI (2000). 'Building a Better Quality of Life: A Strategy for Sustainable Construction' [online]. Available from: http://www.dti. gov.uk/files/file13547.pdf [accessed 27 February 2007].

DTI (2006). *Review of Sustainable Construction.* London: Department of Transport and Industry. www.berr.gov.uk/files/ file34979.pdf [accessed 9 April 2008].

Early C (2006). 'Terrace homes prolong scrap or save dilemma'. *Planning,* 25 August, pp. 9.

Edwards B and Turrent D (Eds) (2000). *Sustainable Housing: Principles and Practice.* London: Taylor & Francis, Abingdon, Oxon.

Egan J (2004). *Skills for Sustainable Communities.* London: Office of the Deputy Prime Minister.

Ellingham I and Fawcett W (2006). *New Generation Whole-life Costing.* London: Taylor & Francis.

Ellison L and Sayce S (2007). 'Assessing sustainability in the existing commercial property stock: establishing sustainability criteria relevant for the commercial property investment sector'. *Property Management,* Vol. 25. No.3 pp.287–304.

Empty Homes Agency (undated). 'VAT' [online]. Available from: www.emptyhomes.com [accessed 20 March 2007].

English Heritage (1998). *Conservation-Led Regeneration: The Work of English Heritage.* London: English Heritage.

English Heritage (2000). *Power of Place.* London: English Heritage.

English Heritage (2003). *Heritage Counts 2003: The State of the Historic Environment.* London: English Heritage.

English Heritage (2004). *Low Demand Housing and the Historic Environment.* London: English Heritage.

English Heritage (2005). *Low Demand Housing: The Case for Conservation-Led Regeneration.* London: English Heritage.

English Heritage (2006). *Climate Change and the Historic Environment.* London: English Heritage.

Environmental Audit Committee (2005). *Housing: Building a Sustainable Future, First Report of Session 2004–05.* London: Environmental Audit Committee.

Ezard J (2004). 'How to recapture cities' civic pride'. *The Guardian* [online], 31 May. Available from: http://arts.guardian.co.uk/news/ story/0,,1228116,00.html [accessed 8 June 2004].

Fuller S (2005). *Life-Cycle Cost Analysis (LCCA)* [online]. Washington: National Institute of Standards and Technology. Available from: http://www.wbdg.org/design/lcca.php?print=1 [accessed 6 March 2006].

Garlick R (2006). 'Agency softens demolition stance'. *Regeneration and Renewal,* 24 March, p. 10.

Girling R (2004). 'Save our streets'. *Sunday Times Magazine* [online], 19 September 2004. Available from: http://www. timesonline.co.uk/tol/life_and_style/article479682.ece [accessed 20 March 2007].

Gordon A (1974). 'The long life/loose fit/low energy study: architects and resource conservation'. *RIBA Journal,* January, pp. 9–12.

Graham B, Ashworth G and Tunbridge J (2000). *A Geography of Heritage.* London: Routledge.

GVA Grimley (2005). *Integration of Middleport Neighbourhood Action Plan with Burslem Town Centre Masterplan and Urban Design Action Plan.* London: RENEW and Stoke-on-Trent City Council.

Haskell T (1993). *Caring for our Built Environment.* London: Spon.

Hemphill L, McGreal S and Berry J (2004a). 'An indicator-based approach to measuring sustainable urban regeneration performance: Part 1, Conceptual foundations and methodological framework'. *Urban Studies,* Vol. 41, No. 4, pp. 725–755.

Hemphill L, McGreal S and Berry J (2004b). 'An indicator-based approach to measuring sustainable urban regeneration performance: Part 2, Empirical evaluation and case-study analysis'. *Urban Studies,* Vol. 41, No. 4, pp. 757–772.

Heritage Link (2004). *The Heritage Dynamo: How the Voluntary Sector Drives Regeneration.* London: Heritage Link.

Heritage Lottery Fund (2004). *New Life and Regeneration.* London: Heritage Lottery Fund.

Hollander J (2002). 'Measuring community: using sustainability indicators'. In Devens MA *Planners' Casebook,* 39, Winter. 1–7.

Holloway D and Bunker R (2006). 'Planning, housing and energy use: a review'. *Urban Policy and Research,* Vol. 24, No. 1, pp. 115–26.

Hope D and Sidebottom M (RENEW North Staffordshire) (2007). Interview. 15 January.

Hunt T (2004). 'Past masters'. *The Guardian (Society* supplement), 2 June, pp. 2–3.

IPD (2002, revised and updated 2006). *The Investment Performance of Listed Office Buildings.* London: Investment Property Databank.

Ireland D (2005). 'The green house effect'. *The Guardian,* 5 May. www.guardian.co.uk/society/2005/may/05/housingpolicy. environment/print [accessed: 4 April 2008].

Jones E, Leach M (2000). Devolving residential energy efficiency responsibility to local government. The case of HECA. *Local Environment,* Vol. 56, pp. 69–81.

Jones E, Wade J, Barton D (2001). Residential sector energy services in the UK: can legislation turn rhetoric into reality? *Impetus consulting.* London. pp. 241–253.

Kilbert C J and Chini Abdol R (2000). *Overview of Deconstruction in Selected Countries.* Rotterdam, The Netherlands: International Council for Research and Innovation in Building Construction.

Kintrea K and Morgan J (2005). 'Evaluation of English Housing Policy – Theme 3 Housing Quality and Neighbourhood Quality' [online]. (London: ODPM.) Available from: www.comunities.gov. uk/documents/housing/pdf/138139 [accessed: 7 April 2008].

Kotval Z (2001). 'Measuring the effectiveness of downtown revitalisation strategies'. Cited in Balsas C J L (2004) 'Measuring the livability of an urban centre: an exploratory study of key performance indicators'. *Planning Practice and Research* Vol. 19, No. 1, pp. 101–110.

Langmaid J (2006). What is whole life cost anaysis? BSRIA Press and information. www.bsria.co.uk/press/?press=815 [14 April 2008].

Larkham P (1996). *Conservation and the City.* London: Routledge.

Likierman A (1993). 'Performance indicators: twenty early lessons from managerial use'. *Public Money and Management.* Vol. 13 No. 4 pp. 15–22.

Lowe R, Bell M (2000). Building regulation and sustainable housing, Part 2: technical issues. *Structural Survey.* Vol. 18, No. 2, pp. 77–88.

Lützkendorf T and Lorenz D (2005). Sustainable property investment: valuing sustainable buildings through property performance assessment. *Building Research & Information* Vol. 33, No. 3, pp. 212–234.

McEvoy D, Gibbs D C and Longhurst J W S (1999). 'The prospects for improved energy efficiency in the UK residential sector'. *Journal of Environmental Planning and Management* Vol. 42, No. 3, pp. 409–424.

Newcastle-under-Lyme Borough Council (2005). *Knutton and Cross Heath AAP: Sustainability Report – Non-technical Summary.*

Northern Way Steering Group (2005). *Moving Forward: The Northern Way (Action Plan – Progress Report).* Newcastle upon Tyne: Northern Way Steering Group.

ODPM (2003a). *English Housing Condition Survey: Key Findings for 2003.* London: Office of the Deputy Prime Minister.

ODPM (2003b). *Sustainable Communities: Building for the Future.* London: Office of the Deputy Prime Minister.

ODPM (2003c). *What Is a Sustainable Community?* [online]. London: Department for Communities and Local Government. Available from: http://www.odpm.gov.uk/Index.asp?Id=1139866 [accessed 20 March 2007].

ODPM (2004). *Housing, Planning, Local Government and the Regions Committee. The Role of Historic Buildings in Urban Regeneration, 2003–04. Vols I & II.* London: Office of the Deputy Prime Minister.

ODPM (2005). *Housing, Planning, Local Government and the Regions Committee. Empty homes and low-demand pathfinders.* Eighth report of session 2004–05 Vol. 1. The Stationery Office. www.parliament.the-stationery-office.co.uk/pa/cm200405/cmselect/cmodpm/295/295.pdf

ODPM (2006). *Market Renewal Pathfinders – Location Map* [online]. London: Department for Communities and Local Government. Available from: www.communities.gov.uk/documents/housing/gif/152311 [accessed 9 April 2008].

Oliver L, Ferber U, Grimski D, Millar K and Nathanail P (2005). 'The scale and nature of European brownfields'. *Proceedings of CABERNET 2005: The International Conference on Managing Urban Land,* Nottingham: www.cabernet.org.uk/resources/417.pdf [accessed 7 April 2008].

Orbasli A (2007). 'The place of heritage in sustainable development'. Paper to conference – *Development and Heritage: The Crucial Balance,* London, 7 March.

Palmer J, Platt S, Fawcett W, Baker N, Brown A and de Carteret R (2003). *Report to the Energy Savings Trust: Refurbish or Replace?* Context Report. Cambridge: Cambridge Architectural Research Ltd.

Park C (1998). 'Sustainable design and historic preservation'. *Cultural Resource Management,* Vol. 21, No. 2, pp. 14–16.

Pickard R and de Thyse M (2001). 'The management of historic centres: towards a common goal'. In R Pickard (ed.) *The Management of Historic Centres.* London: Spon, pp. 274–290.

Pickard R and Pickerill T (2007). *A Review of Fiscal Measures to Benefit Heritage Conservation.* RICS Research Paper Series Vol. 7, No. 6. London: RICS.

Power A (2004). *Sustainable Communities and Sustainable Development: A Review of the Sustainable Communities Plan.* London: SDC.

Power A (2006). *Note for HM Treasury on Neighbourhood Renewal, Housing Repair and VAT* [online]. London: HM Treasury. Available from: www.renewal.net/Documents/MC/Research/TreasuryNote.doc [accessed 20 March 2007].

The Prince's Trust (undated). Regeneration Through Heritage Handbook [online]. Available from: www.princes-regeneration.org/publications.php

RENEW North Staffordshire (2005). *Your Future, Your Say: Middleport* (newsletter), February.

RENEW North Staffordshire (2006a). 'The Project Explained' [online]. Available from: www.renewnorthstaffs.gov.uk/documents/docs/Board%20paper%20summaries/september%202006/Agenda%20item%207E.pdf [accessed 19 January 2007].

RENEW North Staffordshire (2006b). *Your Future, Your Say: Knutton & Cross Heath* (newsletter), May.

RENEW North Staffordshire (2006c). *Reviewing the Use of Neighbourhood Renewal Assessments.* Partnership Board agenda item 7E, 27 September. www.renewnorthstaffs.gov.uk/documents/docs/Board%20paper%20summaries/November%202006/Agenda%20item%207E.pdf

RENEW North Staffordshire (2006d). *Design Issues.* Partnership Board agenda item 7C, 28 November. www.renewnorthstaffs.gov.uk/documents/docs/Board%20paper%20summaries/November%202006/Agenda%20item%207C.pdf

RENEW North Staffordshire (2006e). *Sustainability.* Partnership Board agenda item 7D, 28 November. www.renewnorthstaffs.gov.uk/documents/docs/Board%20paper%20summaries/November%202006/Agenda%20item%207D.pdf

Resurgence (2005). 'Energy Options: Low Energy House' [online]. Available from: http://www.resurgence.org/2005/marriage231.htm [accessed 30 July 2007].

RICS (2004). *Housing Market Renewal: Making the Pathfinders Succeed.* London: Royal Institution of Chartered Surveyors.

RICS (2006). 'DTI Energy Review Our Energy Challenge – Securing Clean Affordable Energy for the Long Term: Comments from The Royal Institution of Chartered Surveyors' [online]. Available from: www.rics.org/NR/rdonlyres/85AE09C7-E5FC-420D-9F9B-A58A63BF145B/10/019BBUKEnergyReview2.doc [accessed 10 June 2006].

Rypkema D (2005). 'Economics, sustainability and historic preservation. A speech at the National Trust for Historic Preservation Annual Conference. Portland, Oregon, 1 October. www.ptvermont.org/rypkema.htm.

Rypkema D (2002). *Historic Preservation and Affordable H.
The Missed Connection.* Washington: The National Trust for
Historic Preservation.

SAVE Britain's Heritage (1998). *Catalytic Conversions.* London:
SAVE.

SAVE Britain's Heritage (undated). 'Pathfinder' [online].
London: SAVE Britain's Heritage. Available from: http://www.
savebritainsheritage.org/main.htm [accessed 13 March 2006].

SFSO (2002). *Measuring Sustainable Development: Insight into
MONET.* Swiss Federal Statistical Office. Neuchâtel.

Stoke-on-Trent City Council (2006). Minutes of Regeneration
Overview & Scrutiny Committee, 14 June.

Sustainable Buildings Task Group (2004). Sustainable buildings
task group report.

Sustainable Construction Task Group (2003). *The UK
Construction Industry: Progress Towards More Sustainable
Construction 2000–2003.* London: Department of Trade and
Industry.

dell S, Oc T and Heath T (1996). *Revitalising Historic Urban
rters.* Oxford: Architectural Press.

URBED and Department of the Environment (1987). *Reusing
Redundant Building,* London: HMSO.

van Bueren E and Priemus H (2002). 'Institutional barriers to
sustainable construction'. *Environment and Planning B,* Vol. 29 (1),
pp. 75–86.

Wain J (2005). A Guide to EcoHomes. An environmental
assessment method for homes. Sustainable Homes.

Waters M (2006). *Environmental Sustainability: Is it HIP?.* Reading:
The College of Estate Management.

Waters M and Karadimitriou N (2006). *Urban Blights to Northern
Lights? The Effect of Autonomous Speculative Investment in
UK Housing Market Renewal Areas.* Reading: College of Estate
Management.

Yates T (2006). *Sustainable Refurbishment of Victorian Housing:
Guidance, Assessment Method and Case Studies.* Watford:
IHS BRE Press.